How The West Was Won

THE
COWBOYS

Skyhorse Publishing

How The West Was Won

THE
COWBOYS

BRUCE WEXLER

Skyhorse Publishing

Skyhorse Publishing books may be purchased in bulk at
special discounts for sales promotion, corporate gifts,
fund-raising, or educational purposes. Special editions can
also be created to specifications. For details, contact the
Special Sales Department, Skyhorse Publishing,
307 West 36th Street, 11th Floor, New York, NY 10018 or
"mailto:info@skyhorsepublishing.com"info@skyhorsepublishing.com.

Skyhorse® and Skyhorse Publishing® are registered
trademarks of Skyhorse Publishing, Inc.®,
a Delaware corporation.

www.skyhorsepublishing.com

10 9 8 7 6 5 4 3 2 1

Library of Congress Cataloging-in-Publication Data TK

ISBN: 978-1-61608-573-5

Printed in China

Contents

Introduction

The proud tradition of American cowboying has a very long history that dates right back to the Mexican charros. They, in turn, inherited their skills from the Spanish *conquistadors*, who had arrived in the Americas following Christopher Columbus's discovery of the New World in 1492.

Opposite page: The cowboy has become a classic character in American folklore.

The heyday of the American cowboy stretched from the years following the Civil War through to the 1880s. This was the time of the great cattle drives along the iconic cattle trails. These acted as arteries of cow commerce from the Southern states to America's meat-hungry East and North. The impetus behind the growing cattle trade was simple: there were more cattle than people in the huge tract of land between the Great Plains and California, while the industrialised and heavily-populated northern and eastern states were crying out for fresh meat.

Inevitably, this led to a great increase in the number of men employed in the industry. Although cowhands had been working on ranches in Georgia and Florida before the Civil War, the profession only became familiar to most Americans when they became familiar in the states and territories to the west of the Missouri. In the decades following the war, it is estimated that as many as forty-thousand men worked as cow punchers in the burgeoning cattle industry.

The term "cowboy" itself is thought to have been coined by the greatest cattleman of all, Charles Goodnight. When Goodnight wrote about the ranching methods he used on his extensive J.A. Ranch, he explained how he had employed "a little army of men called "cowboys"" to care for his hundred-thousand head of cattle. Surprisingly, Goodnight was writing in the mid 1880s, when land enclosure was already threatening the cowhand's traditional role. Goodnight had originally referred to his hands as "boys," and he did indeed have a very paternal relationship with them. At this time, the average age of a western cowboy was around twenty-four.

It could be argued that far from being free to roam the unspoiled prairie, cowboys were actually little more than servants of investors from eastern America and Europe as the cattle business became hugely profitable. But despite this, our image of the brave cowboy persists, that of a strong and resolute individual facing down dangers of all kinds; wild weather, wild beasts, and wild men.

The involvement of capital, especially in the railroad industry, did have a huge effect on the cattle trade. Immensely long cattle drives were now required to bring cattle from the Texan and Southern ranches to the railheads that had sprung up, mostly in Kansas. From here, the animals were loaded onto cattle trucks and shipped to where their meat could bring the highest prices. Generally, this was about ten times what the meat was worth in the South.

The cowboys themselves led tough and largely thankless lives, surviving on meagre pay of around $25 to $45 a month. Few were literate, and most would have struggled to find other forms of employment. Their work was also dangerous; every cowboy had to beware of stampedes, snakes, and drought, but a cowboy's most likely cause of death was from riding accidents. It was relatively common for men to be dragged, thrown, or kicked to death by their own horse. The second most likely cause of death was from pneumonia, hardly surprising when you consider their working and living conditions.

Though it may seem lonely and unrewarding by modern standards, the life of the cowboy seems to carry lasting appeal. We admire their courage and self-reliance, and their freedom to roam across the unspoiled wilderness of the West. The cowboy has become a true icon of the American way of life.

The History of The Cowboy

Oh, he would twirl that lariat and he didn't do it slow
He could catch them forefeet nine out of ten for any kind of dough
And when the herd stamped he was always on the spot
And set them to milling, like the stirrings of a pot

— from Zebra Dun, cowboy folk song

Opposite page: For many Americans, John Wayne is the epitome of cowboy glamor. In real life, he was admired for his horsemanship and courage.

Of all the West's iconic characters, the cowboy is the most universally recognized and admired. But the cowboy role that has come to symbolize the free spirit of America actually originated in Spain. When the conquistadors imported their cattle handling skills into South America in the sixteenth century, the vaqueros learned how to herd large numbers of horses and cattle across the open lands to forage. These original cowpunchers were usually mounted on horseback, but also rode donkeys, or burros. The Spanish were also responsible for bringing the first Longhorn cattle to America in 1493.

The word "cowboy" (the English-language equivalent of the Spanish vaqueros), made its first appearance between 1715 and 1725. By this time, the cattle industry had become an important element of the North American economy, particularly in the South and West. The "boy" tag was not meant to be demeaning; tough work like this required youth and vigor, and boys as young as twelve were employed in ranch work.

As European settlers imported Longhorn cattle to America, a culture of ranching became established, particularly in the South. Surprisingly, the market for beef meat was very limited at this time, and the animals were mainly bred for their hides and tallow. The State of Texas (independent from 1836), soon became prominent in the American cattle trade. Anglo-Texans drove out many Mexican ranchers from the territory and confiscated their animals. This new breed of Texas cattlemen soon developed its own cowboy traditions. Typically the Texas cowboy was a solitary drifter, who worked for a different outfit every season.

Ranching had been established much longer in California. There were already nineteen rancheros by 1790, and this number was greatly increased by 1836. Spanish mission farmlands were often seized by the Mexican government and huge

Above: A romantic evocation of the life of a cowboy. One man and his horse guard the herd, while the others rest in their dreaming sacks.

Right: The heyday of the cattle trails was between 1866 and 1890.

tracts of land were redistributed to favored ranchers for grazing. More verdant grazing meant that there was less open range, and Californian meat tended to stay in the region. This meant far fewer cattle drives, and more settled living conditions for Californian cowboys, who mostly lived on permanent ranches. Also known as buckaroos, they were considered more skilled in animal husbandry than their Texan counterparts. California cowboys often aspired to someday own their own ranches, get married, and have a family, whereas Texan cowboys were far more likely to stay single and wander the land.

A third type of cowhand, known as the Florida cowhunter, or "cracker cowboy", had a completely different way of working. Spanish settlers had introduced cattle to the state in the sixteenth century, and cowhunters were usually of Spanish or American Indian descent. These men used dogs and bullwhips rather than horses

Right: A small number of well-trained cowboys could control thousands of cows on the trail. They were paid between $25 and $40 a month for their hard work.

Opposite page: Roping was an important skill for a trailhand, and became celebrated in rodeos across the West.

Below: The tough and distinctive Texas Longhorn was well-suited to the cattle drives. The breed lost very little weight along the trail.

and lassos to control the smaller breeds of cattle native to this region. Historically, meat produced in Florida was used to supply the Spanish missions in the north of the state and the island of Cuba, but this meat became of critical importance to the Confederacy during the Civil War. It was so crucial that in March, 1864, the eight-hundred-strong Cow Cavalry (the 1st Battalion Florida Special Cavalry) was formed to protect the cattle from Union raiders.

In Canada, the cattle industry was focused on Alberta and Saskatchewan. Many cowboys working in Canada came north from America. Elsewhere in the Americas, Hawaii had its paniolos, Argentina its gauchos, Peru its chalans, Chile its huasos, and Mexico its vaqueros and charros. Each of these regions had wide-open spaces for grazing cattle, sheep, or horses, and developed its own special herding techniques and traditions.

A fantastic panorama of a cattle drive. The photograph shows the ethnic diversity of the trailhands.

Marlin Models 1893 and 1894

Winchester didn't have it all its own way in the Western market. The Marlin Firearms Company launched its first lever-action rifle in 1881, followed by the Model 1893. The 1893 was the company's first rifle designed for the recently introduced smokeless cartridge. It was offered in five different calibers. The barrels were either round or octagonal, and varied in length between twenty-four and thirty-two inches. Some 900,000 examples of the gun were manufactured. They were marked Model 1893 up to 1905 but this was shortened to Model 93 thereafter. This example is marked Model 93.

The Model 1894 was very similar to the Model 1893, but had a shorter action. This example is in .25-20 caliber and has a twenty-four inch round barrel. Marlin manufactured around 250,000 Model 1894s between 1894 and 1935. Marlin guns were mass-produced and sold at competitive prices. Their marketing strategy is the same today. As a result, the Marlin was a popular cowboy weapon.

John M. Marlin founded Marlin Firearms in 1870.

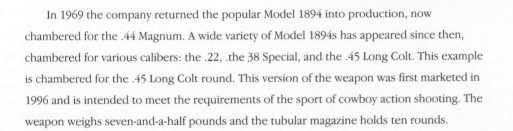

Marlin's 1893 was their first rifle specifically designed for the smokeless cartridge.

In 1969 the company returned the popular Model 1894 into production, now chambered for the .44 Magnum. A wide variety of Model 1894s has appeared since then, chambered for various calibers: the .22, .the 38 Special, and the .45 Long Colt. This example is chambered for the .45 Long Colt round. This version of the weapon was first marketed in 1996 and is intended to meet the requirements of the sport of cowboy action shooting. The weapon weighs seven-and-a-half pounds and the tubular magazine holds ten rounds.

The original Marlin workshop was located on State Street in New Haven, Connecticut.

SPECIFICATIONS

Caliber: .22, .38 Special, .45 Long Colt

Barrel: 24-32 inches

Type: Lever-action repeating rifle

Origin: Marlin Firearms Co., New Haven, Connecticut

The Cattle Towns of the West

Below: Cattle were loaded onto eastbound trains at the cattle town rail heads.

The defeat of the Southern states in the Civil War had a great effect on the cattle industry, leading to a kind of cowboy diaspora. When Texans went off to fight in the war, their cattle were left to roam free, and huge herds built up. After the war, there was no market for the five million cattle stranded in the economically crippled South, while the wealthy and industrial North was desperate for meat.

To drive these cattle north was extremely difficult, time-consuming, and dangerous. This meant that cowboy skills were in high demand. Originally, the Texan herds were driven across Missouri on their way to the north and east. But the cattlemen ran into increasing hostility from the local farmers, who objected to the damage that the cattle drives caused. Many also believed that the cows carried a virulent tick that was deadly to their livestock. In effect, this standoff meant that thousands of cattle were marooned in Texas, where they were worth only $4 a head. They were prevented from reaching the North, where each animal was worth in excess of $40.

This economic opportunity was the impetus that inspired an economically and culturally important phenomenon. This was a completely new kind of settlement, the western cattle town.

These towns underwent a boom that lasted for about five years. The major cattle towns were all at the new Kansas railheads: Abilene, Hays City, Dodge City, Newton, and Ellsworth.

Above: It wasn't long before the cow towns had the veneer
of respectability and all the usual amenities.

Abilene, Kansas

Right: Abilene, Kansas in 1879. Most of the town's original buildings were false-fronted wooden structures, but these were gradually replaced by more solid brick buildings.

Abilene was the first of the cow towns of the West. The town began as a small prairie village along the Smoky Hill Trail. Timothy Hersey established it as a stage coach stop in 1857 and gave the town its name, a biblical term that means "city of the plains." At this time, the settlement was no more than a collection of a few wooden huts, but boom times were coming. Texan cattle men had been searching for a safe and accessible market for their wild Texas Longhorn cattle, but did not find themselves welcome anywhere. This staggering economic opportunity was not lost on entrepreneurial cattlemen like Illinois businessman Joseph G. McCoy. He had a vision of a great cattle depot on the plains, from which cattle could be shipped by train to the industrial East.

McCoy persuaded the Kansas Pacific Railroad to build a siding at Abilene, Kansas. In 1867 he opened his Great Western Stockyards at Abilene's railhead, where cattle could be held before being loaded onto the eastbound railroad. McCoy's stockyards were the largest ones west of Kansas City, and were perfectly situated right next to grazing prairies. He then encouraged the Texas ranchers to drive their animals to Abilene. In 1867, the first year of Abilene's great cattle market, McCoy was responsible for shipping 35,000 head of cattle eastwards. By 1871, this had increased to 600,000 animals shipped on the hoof.

Overleaf: A panoramic view of Abilene's High Street. Its dirt road gives way to the open prairie in the very near distance.

In this way, Abilene became the first major end-of-the-line town, situated at the head of the Chisholm Cattle Trail. The town boomed, and the local hotel — The Drovers Cottage — became the headquarters of the cattle bosses and buyers from the East. By 1868, the town's population had swelled with an influx of cowboys, gamblers, pimps, prostitutes, and gunslingers. The usual trouble ensued, and galloping horses

and the sound of wild gunplay became commonplace on Abilene's streets. It soon became one of the wildest towns in the West, and remained so for a couple of years.

Joseph McCoy wrote that these newcomers would "imbibe too much poison whiskey and straightway go on the warpath... At such times it is not safe to be on

Above: McCoy opened his Abilene stockyards in 1867. The Kansas Pacific Railroad shipped thousands of cattle east from here.

the streets." The Devil's Addiction district of the town was particularly riotous.

By the spring of 1870, the townsfolk of Abilene had had enough of this violence, and decided to suppress it with a newly-appointed marshal and a "no guns" law. But the cowboys came into town as usual, ripped up the anti-gun notice, and demolished the newly built jail. Abilene's civic leaders then tried to employ two police officers from St. Louis, Missouri; legend has it that the two men rode the train into town, took one look around, and returned to St. Louis the same evening.

A man of a much higher caliber arrived later that year, when Marshal Tom "Bear River" Smith rode into town on his famous mount, Silverheels. Smith enforced the "no guns" policy with his bare hands. Smith survived two assassination attempts, but was ultimately murdered and decapitated on November 2, 1870, after just a few months on the job. In April, 1871 Abilene turned to Wild Bill Hickok in the hope that his reputation would bring some order to the town. Hickok's period in office ended ignominiously when he accidentally shot and killed his own deputy, Mike Williams. He was fired from the Abilene job in December that year.

But by the fall of 1871 the tracks had been extended, and the cattle trade was already moving on from Abilene to other Kansas rail towns further along the line, such as Ellsworth, Hays City, Newton, and Dodge City.

Ellsworth, Kansas

Ellsworth was known as "The Wickedest Cattletown in Kansas." Of all the cattle towns, it was said that "Abilene, [was] the first, Dodge City, the last, but Ellsworth the wickedest." The town was named for the nearby Fort Ellsworth, which had been constructed in 1864. In the 1860s, the new Kansas Pacific stockyards at the railhead meant that Ellsworth became a bustling cowtown, filled with cowboys and trail bosses. The railroad cut the town's main street in two. The cattle bosses had pretty much abandoned Abilene by 1872, and Ellsworth took over the business. Like Abilene, Ellsworth became redolent with violence, and the streets rang with the sound of gunfire. Shootings became so commonplace that it was said that "Ellsworth had a man every morning for breakfast." Most of the town businesses were run for cowboys: saloons (including the famous Plaza), dancehalls (including Lizzie Palmer's), gambling halls, and brothels. There was also a famous drovers'

Below: The Kansas Pacific Railroad extended the train line and, by 1872, the cattle business had moved from Abilene to Ellsworth.

Left: The Southwestern Hotel in Caldwell, Kansas. Though not as famous as some of the larger cow towns, Caldwell's position on the Chisholm Trail kept the cattle drives coming between 1871 and 1885.

Above: Ellsworth in 1871. J. Mueller's shop catered for the footwear needs of cowboys driving cattle to the town.

mercantile store — the Old Reliable House — that sold cowboy supplies, clothing, and equipment. Cowboys passing through the town also bought gifts at the store to take home to their families in Texas.

In 1872, Ellsworth's Drover's Cottage Hotel (which had moved there from Abilene) opened, with rooms for one-hundred-seventy-five guests. It was used by trail bosses and stockmen. The transient nature of the town meant that violence was commonplace. Ellsworth's resident population was only 448 people in 1870; by 1880 it had more than doubled to 929. One of the main reasons that genuine settlers avoided Ellsworth was the town's lawless character and bad reputation. Wild Bill Hickok ran for town marshal in 1868, but was beaten to the post by ex-soldier E. W. Kingsbury. Although popular and well-respected, Kingsbury struggled to control the town, even with the help of the local police force. On September 26, 1869 Marshal Will Semans was shot and killed in Joe Brennan's saloon. An outbreak of serious mayhem followed, as the local criminals took advantage of the vacuum in law enforcement. Two local miscreants, known only as Craig and Johnson, were particularly active in terrorizing the town. In the end, they pushed the Ellsworth townsfolk too hard; a group of local vigilantes caught up with and lynched the pair near the Smoky Hill River.

Another famous lawman, Wyatt Earp, worked in Ellsworth briefly. The town's violence and lawlessness came to a head in 1873, when a drunken Billy Thompson accidentally shot and killed Ellsworth County Sheriff Chauncey Whitney. This killing launched a tide of violence, during which it was said that "Hell was in session at Ellsworth." Although Thompson was acquitted of murder, Whitney's killing led to a great deal of hostility towards cowboys, which culminated in a double tragedy. Chief of Police Ed Crawford pistol-whipped Texan cowboy Cad Pierce to death. A short while later, Crawford himself was shot to death in a local brothel. It was assumed that this shooting was a revenge killing for Pierce's death. This tide of violence led to several other shootings, including those of ex-Marshal "Happy" Jack Morco and Texan Ed Crawford.

As the trails began to favor other Kansas towns, Ellsworth's crime rate dropped, but so did the economic activity in the town. Kansas Pacific finally shut down its Ellsworth shipping pens in 1875.

Below: Wichita, Kansas. The ramshackle shops catered to all a cowboy's needs.

Left: This gun shop in Denver, Colorado, sold and repaired firearms for cowboys.

Sharps Buffalo Rifle

The Sharps Buffalo rifle was a legend in the West and had a fearsome reputation. Its long-distance accuracy and tremendous stopping power is celebrated in a classic Hollywood movie scenario. The bad guy confidently rides off into the sunset, while the good guy takes aim unhurriedly. He touches the foresight with spit to provide a gleam of light, and adjusts the vernier backsight. When the good guy squeezes the trigger, the audience is convinced that his adversary has escaped. As it is fired, the Sharps rifle booms loudly. The barrel bucks from the explosive detonation of the heavy .50 cartridge, then silence returns. We watch the bad guy continue his ride into the distance for several long, tantalizing seconds. Suddenly, almost in slow motion, the shot connects with bad man's retreating form. Dead, he slumps from his mount.

Such drama seldom entered the life of an ordinary trail cowboy. His requirements were for a heavy caliber rifle that could bring down large game for the chuck wagon, or a sick steer at considerable distance. The gun could also be used to warn off trouble. The booming report from its large caliber ammunition had an strong deterrent effect on anyone planning to harm the herd.

Sharps Rifle Manufacturing Company was founded by Christian Sharps on October 9, 1851.

This example has a classic thirty-inch barrel. It is smaller than the big .50, but at .45-70, it is still an extremely potent weapon. The .45 lead slug was propelled by a seventy grain charge. Even the standard Winchester at only .44-40 (with forty grains at its disposal) was a mighty gun. The .50 Sharps was simply devastating.

The gun pictured was supplied by J.P. Lower of Denver, the famous western dealer and outfitter. His name is stamped on top of the barrel. The gun has double set triggers and a shotgun butt plate. It also has Lower's special Rocky Mountain buckhorn site that he designed himself, and had made up by Sharps. The tang site is a modified sporting site with a vernier staff added for extra range. The gun was known as "old reliable."

The company was finally dissolved in 1881, but replicas of their famous guns are still made today.

SPECIFICATIONS

Caliber: .45 to .70

Barrel: 30 inch octagonal

Finish: Blue casehardened

Grips: Walnut

Action: Single-shot, breech loading

Hays City, Kansas

Just as in Abilene and Ellsworth, it was the building of the Kansas Pacific Railway that inspired the foundation of Hays City. The entrepreneurial Buffalo Bill Cody and the railroad contractor William Rose founded the settlement of Rome, Kansas, near Fort Hays. The fort had been established to protect railroad constructors from Indian attack. Cody and Rose hoped that the railroad would come to their fledgling town. A rival developer to Cody and Rose, Dr. William Webb, established an alternative settlement on the other bank of the Big Creek. This new town was called Hays City. The railroad bosses favoured Hays City for the end of the new tracks, and Cody and Rose's venture failed. As soon as the railroad reached the new municipality in 1867, Hays City grew rapidly. By the following year, Rome, Kansas, was a ghost town.

As an end-of-the-line town, Hays became the supply point for the territories to the west and southwest. The town was soon full of businesses, including the Gibbs House hotel, the Moses and Bloomfield general store, and a post office. Most of the early town buildings were wooden frame structures, but a stone drugstore soon graced the town. Hays City soon had its first newspaper, appropriately named the Railway Advance.

Just like Abilene and Ellsworth, Hays City was beset by crime and violence from its foundation. This was largely a side effect of the town's role as a railhead for cattle being shipped east. It was also the outfitting station for the wagon trains following the Smoky Hill Trail eastward. As well as the usual casual violence, desperados like Jim Curry also plagued the town. During his stay he murdered several black men, a few townsfolk, and a young boy. Soldiers from the local fort were also involved in violence in Hays City. George and Elizabeth Custer lived at Fort Hays for a while, and Elizabeth wrote that "there was enough desperate history in that little town to make a whole library of dime novels."

Above: Cattle were branded to show their owner's mark. This allowed cattle from several ranches to graze together.

Between 1867 and 1873, more than thirty people were murdered in the town, necessitating the establishment of the famous Boot Hill Cemetery in Hays City. In 1869, Elizabeth Custer noted that there were already thirty-six graves there. Law enforcement was a priority, and Wild Bill Hickok served as town marshal for a few months in 1869. Unfortunately, his effect on the town was less than benign. He managed to kill two townsmen, two soldiers, and wound several others during his employment at Hays City. He was forced to flee the town and was next heard of working in Abilene.

By 1872, the railroad had been built to Dodge City, and the cattle industry had pretty much abandoned Hays City. The town began to establish itself as the center of a farming community, and the trouble moved on to Dodge City.

In 1873, a stone courthouse was erected in Hays City, and a schoolhouse was built by a subscription that raised twelve thousand dollars. In 1875, local luminary H. P. Wilson built an elegant stone residence on Chestnut Street, the Pennsylvania House. Civilization had made it to Hays City.

Newton, Kansas

On July 17, 1871, the Atchison, Topeka and Santa Fe Railroad arrived at Newton. The town was the railhead for the famous Chisholm Trail, the shipping point for the huge herds that has previously been loaded onto the railroad at Abilene. Newton was incorporated as a city of the third class in 1872. The coming of the

Above: Dodge City became known as "the Queen of Cow Towns". The cattle industry moved there when a spur from the Chisholm Trail (which became known as the Great Western Cattle Trail) was diverted to the town. The town's peak years in the cattle trade were 1883 and 1884.

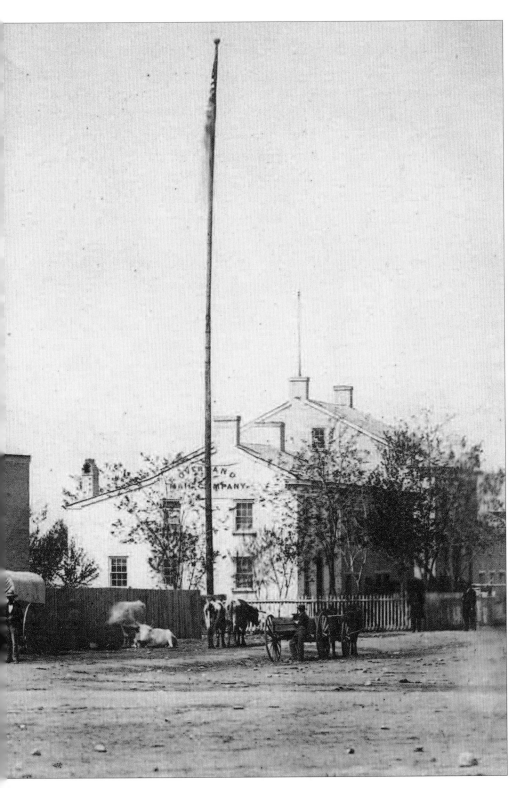

Previous pages: Salt Lake City became a hub of the Utah cattle industry from the 1850s onwards. Many Mormons became cowboys.

Left: Once the railroads had been built, Utah cattle drovers herded their animals to the railhead at Salt Lake City.

railroad and the cattle drives attracted the usual cast of desperados: gunslingers, gamblers, and prostitutes. The town soon rivalled Ellsworth for bloody violence and lawlessness; it, too, was sometimes called the "wickedest city in the West." Newton's bad reputation was largely due to the notorious gunfight that took place on August 9, 1871 in Perry Tuttle's dance house in the Hyde Park area of the town. Eight men were shot to death in the fracas. Despite this, the town soon became well known for its hospitality. The Hyde Park area boasted fifteen different saloons, included the Do Drop In, The Side Track, and the Gold Rooms.

When the railway moved on to Dodge City in 1872, complete with a branch line to Wichita, the cattle trade moved on with it, and Newton was freed from many of the rough types that had frequented its streets. The reign of the cowboy was over, and the first stirrings of law and order were felt in the town. Unfortunately, Newton's tough times weren't over. A terrible fire occurred on the night of December 8, 1873. The east side of block 38 (the business area of the city) was completely destroyed. The population of the town decreased dramatically in the years following 1872, and did not recover until late in that decade.

Dodge City, Kansas

Dodge City dates from 1871, when Henry L. Sitler built a three-room sod house near Fort Dodge. Conveniently located near the Santa Fe Trail, and with the Santa Fe Railroad rapidly approaching from the east, the town started to boom in 1872, and was to become the Queen of the Cow Towns. The Atchison, Topeka, and Santa Fe Railroad arrived in Dodge City in September 1872. A new cattle trail, the Great Western, branched off from the Chisholm Trail to bring cattle to the railhead, and thousands of cattle were soon passing through the town's stockyards. The peak years of the trade were between 1883 and 1884. George M. Hoover opened the town's first saloon, and the town soon boasted the usual selection of saloons (including the Long Branch), gambling halls, barbers, restaurants, general stores, dance halls, and brothels (including the China Doll). The town even had a bullfighting ring for a brief period in 1884. All of these places of entertainment were designed to take as much money as possible from the cowboys that passed through the town. By 1877, nineteen establishments in the town were licensed to sell liquor.

Dodge City started out as a tent town, and its first trade was in buffalo hides and meat. A good hunter could make a hundred dollars a day. These commodities were loaded into railcars and shipped east. An estimated 1,500,000 buffalo hides were shipped from Dodge City between 1872 and 1878. Businesses such as Robert Wright's Dodge City Hide Yard were very profitable, but indiscriminate hunting meant that the prairie was littered with the rotting corpses of dead animals. The mass slaughter destroyed the huge buffalo herds of the plains. Filthy buffalo hunters and traders filled the town's establishments, and inspired the derogatory term "stinker." Longhorn cattle were the next source of income for the town, and were the main source of business for Dodge City for a period of ten years. Over five million head of cattle were driven through the town on their way to the railroad.

Like all the frontier towns, Dodge City passed through a blazing period of violence and lawlessness. There was no conventional law enforcement in the town, and the number of shooting deaths soon necessitated a local graveyard. (Another) Boot Hill Cemetery was established soon after the town was, and saw continuous use until 1878.

Law and order finally arrived in the town with Bat Masterson, Ed Masterson, Wyatt Earp, Bill Tilghman, and Charlie Bassett. An ordinance was passed that guns could not be worn or carried north of the railroad tracks. These tough law enforcers were especially needed in the summer months when cowboys, cattle buyers, gamblers, and prostitutes flooded the town.

Dodge City was the last of the frontier cattle towns. Fort Dodge was closed in 1882, and the cattle drives ended after the notorious blizzard of January 1886. Tired of the itinerant cowboy population, Dodge City had been advertising for permanent settlers since 1874. At that time, the town had consisted of over seventy buildings, including a school. The settlement of the last of the cattle towns marked the end of the Old West.

The Great Cattle Trails

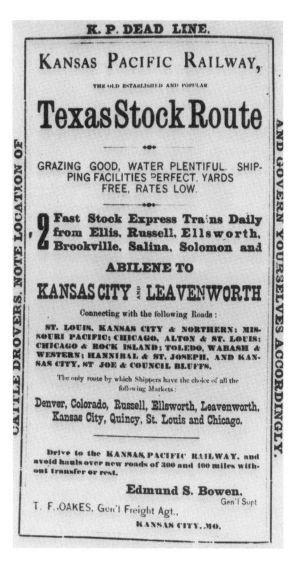

Various trails, or cattle drovers' routes, were chiselled out of the difficult and dangerous landscape to get cattle to the new railhead towns.

The Chisholm Cattle Trail

One of the main routes that the drovers used to get stock from the Texas ranches to McCoy's Abilene stockyards was the Chisholm Cattle Trail. This famous dirt track was named for Jesse Chisholm. Chisholm was born around 1805 in the Hiwassee region of Texas. His father was a slave trader of Scottish descent, and his mother was a Cherokee woman. After his parents separated, Chisholm was brought up in the Cherokee Nation. Before the Civil War broke out (in which he supported the Confederacy), Chisholm had built several trading posts along what was to become the Oklahoma section of the trail. Chisholm's friendship with the plains tribes and his ability to speak fourteen Indian dialects fluently was essential to the opening of the route. Sadly, Chisholm died from food poisoning from eating rancid bear meat in 1868, and never had an opportunity to drive his cattle along the route that still bears his name.

In fact, the first cattleman to use the Chisholm Trail from San Antonio to the railhead at Abilene, Kansas was O. W. Wheeler (together with his two partners, Wilson and Hicks) in 1867. At this time, Abilene itself was only a six-year-old hamlet. Wheeler succeeded in herding 2,400 steers along the route. Ultimately, Chisholm's dirt track was to be trodden by upwards of five million cattle and one million mustangs. It was served by hundreds of smaller feed trails that drew herds from all over Texas, and became an important financial artery for the region. The trail greatly stimulated the cattle trade and helped the South to recover from the devastation of the Civil War.

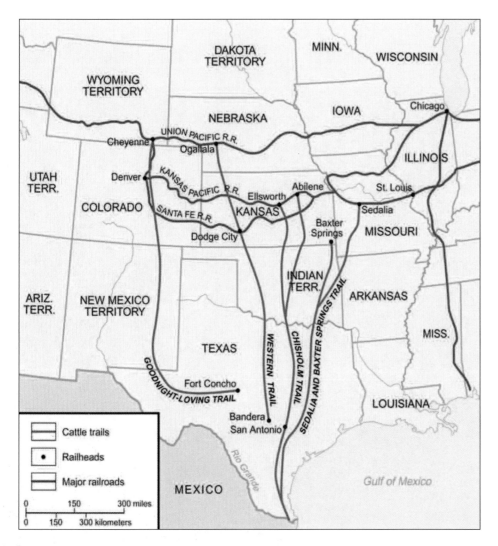

Left: This map shows the cattle trails feeding into the cow town rail heads. They all begin in Texas.

Opposite page: The Kansas Pacific Railway operated between 1863 and 1880. The company operated long-distance lines that were instrumental in opening up the central Great Plains to settlement. Its line from Kansas City to Denver completed the final link in the coast-to-coast railroad in 1870.

In its original form, the Chisholm Trail began in San Antonio, and ended at Abilene. But it was gradually extended further into Kansas; first to Newton, then Wichita, and finally to Caldwell by 1883. The long drive from Texas to Kansas took between two and three months, and was enough to challenge even the most experienced Texas cattlemen. The cattle moved along at around ten to twelve miles a day, which allowed them to graze as they went. The terrain itself was extremely difficult. The herdsmen had to drive the cattle across two major rivers (the Arkansas and the Red), and negotiate various creeks, canyons, mountains, and badlands along the route. Ruthless cattle rustlers and territorial Indians were enough to worry even the most fearless cowboy. At the time, Oklahoma was still part of the Indian Territory. There was also the ever-present danger of stampede

Right: Thirsty cattle raising dust as they swarm to drink. The cattle trails were designed to take advantage of rivers and streams where the herd could be watered.

from the capricious Texan Longhorn. The mastering of these diverse problems greatly enhanced the reputation of the Texas cowboy, and he achieved an almost folkloric status. Specialist trailing contractors managed most of these drives, and they recruited bands of cowboys to ride the line. Over the years, these trail bosses perfected an economic system of cattle driving that meant they could get the animals to market for around sixty to seventy-five cents a head. This was far cheaper than sending the cattle by rail. These highly skilled professional drovers included rugged individuals like John T. Lyle, George W. Slaughter, and the Pryor brothers.

The Great Western Cattle Trail

Also known as the Dodge City Trail and the Old Texas Trail, the Great Western Cattle Trail ran roughly parallel to the Chisholm Trail to the west. Its route began in Bandera, Texas, then passed near to Abilene, Texas, and concluded at Dodge City, Kansas. At the time, Dodge City was the cattle capital of the world. The trail was two thousand miles long and ran mostly through Oklahoma. Feeder trails merged into it from several other areas, including the Rio Grande, Wyoming, and Montana.

Famously, Doan's Crossing was the last supply post on the Great Western Cattle Trail before the lands of the Indian Nation. C. E. Doan was the proprietor of the trading post there, and he kept a tally of the beasts moving through. According to

Below: Trailsmen often lost a few head of cattle to Indian rustlers.

Doan, the peak of the traffic occurred between 1874 and 1886, when five million animals passed along the trail. In 1881, 301,000 head of cattle passed through Doan's Crossing. The largest individual herd to pass through consisted of ten thousand animals. The motivation for driving the cattle along the Great Western Trail was clear. In Texas at this time, cattle were worth ten to twelve dollars a head. In Dodge City, each animal could be sold for around twenty-five dollars. But the trail became increasingly dangerous as the Cheyenne and Arapaho tribes were confined to reservations. Now that the wild antelope and buffalo were nearly extinct, being restricted to these virtually meatless lands effectively meant a lingering death by starvation for the Indians. They tried to survive by demanding a trail bounty of beef from each passing herd. If the trail bosses refused to pay, the Indians retaliated by attacking the drive, or making the cattle stampede (back when the buffalo were plentiful, the Indians would make them stampede over cliffs to kill many animals quickly and easily.)

Opposite page: A cowboy readies his long, knotted *reata* to rope a cow.

Colt Single-Action Army Revolver 1873

The Colt single-action army revolver is one of the greatest handguns in history. Many examples were purchased by the U.S. Army, and the gun was also widely sold on the civilian market. It was particularly popular in the West, where it came to symbolize the cowboy era. The gun dates from 1872, when the U.S. Army held a competition for a new revolver design. The contest was won by Colt. Their entry was accepted for service as the Model 1873 and remained in continuous production for sixty-seven years (between 1873 and 1940). During this time, exactly 357,859 examples were manufactured. The gun was reintroduced into production in 1956. Colt continues to produce small numbers of this revolver, which now carry a high price tag.

There is nothing particularly unusual about the design and construction of the Model 1873, but the inspired combination of simplicity, ruggedness, ease of use, and dependability has made for an enduring and unpretentious classic.

These pearl grips were
probably fitted to the gun
by L.D. Nimschke.

SPECIFICATIONS

Caliber: 44.40 and .45 Colt

Barrel: 4¾, 5½, or 7½ inches

Type: : Single-action, centerfire
revolver

Origin: Colt PFA Mfg Co.,
Hartford, Connecticut

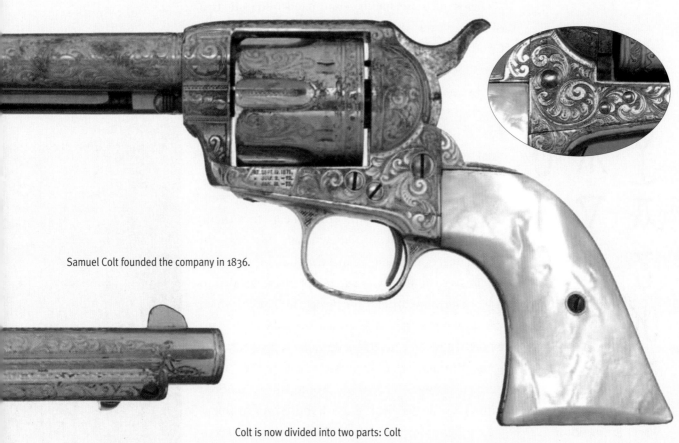

Samuel Colt founded the company in 1836.

Colt is now divided into two parts: Colt
Defense (which serves the military) and the
Colt Manufacturing Company.

The basic Model 1873 was originally produced in three barrel lengths: four and three-quarter, five-and-a-half, and seven-and-a-half inches.

Almost since firearms were invented, owners have had a desire for decorated weapons. As in this case, some of these decorations are truly spectacular. This gun began life as a standard Colt single-action army with a five-inch barrel and it is chambered for the 44-40 caliber round. It bears serial number 89332 and records show that it left the Colt factory in 1883. It was then passed to an engraving shop, almost certainly that of L.D. Nimschke. The gun may even be the work of the master himself. Over ninety percent of the available area of the metalwork has been covered with the most intricate patterns, and even the trigger guard is embellished with cross-hatching. The grips are pearl and fit the weapon perfectly.

Above: Each brand was unique to a particular ranch. Rustlers used ingenious methods to change and disguise them.

The Goodnight-Loving Trail

Perhaps the most famous and romanticized cattle trail of them all was the Goodnight-Loving Trail. Charles Goodnight and Oliver Loving formed a partnership when they met in 1866 and started a cattle drive from Young County in Texas to Fort Sumner, New Mexico.

The original purpose of the Goodnight-Loving Trail was to drive cattle to Fort Sumner in Texas. Eight-thousand Navajo Indians were confined there, virtually starving for want of meat. These tribesmen were the responsibility of government agents, who were desperately trying to procure meat for them. Goodnight and Loving knew that this was an exceptional opportunity to make money.

To avoid an Indian attack, the partners decided to drive their herd around the Texas Panhandle, which was teeming with hostile Comanche tribesmen. This involved taking a much longer and completely arid route through what Goodnight called the "most desolate country". Along the route, three-hundred cattle died in the heat and a hundred more thirst-crazed beasts drowned in a stampede at the Pecos River. Goodnight sold half of the surviving herd to the reservation agents. He then continued the drive into Colorado, selling the remaining animals in Denver. The whole escapade netted the partners the huge sum of $24,000, and the reputation for forging the most famous trail route of all time. In the spring of the

following year, Loving and Goodnight returned to Texas to start a new drive. Loving went ahead to scout the trail through Indian country, with just a trusted scout for company. Although he had promised Goodnight to proceed with extreme caution and to move only under cover of darkness, Loving was overcome with impatience and broke cover during the day. Almost inevitably, this led to an attack by the Comanche tribe, in which Loving was seriously wounded. He somehow managed to make his way back to Fort Sumner, only to die there of gangrene. Goodnight sat by the bedside of his close friend for two weeks, until Loving finally expired.

Goodnight kept a promise he had made to Loving and saw to it that his body was buried in Texas. Goodnight described his partner as "one of the coolest and bravest men I have ever known, but devoid of caution."

The Goodnight-Loving Trail originally ran southwest to the Horsehead Crossing on the Pecos River to Fort Sumner. But in 1871, Goodnight extended the route to join up with the Fort Worth and Denver City Railroad at Grenada, Colorado. From here, many cattle were sold to hungry gold diggers. Ultimately, the trail went as far as Cheyenne, Wyoming.

A traditional scene that has hardly changed from the early days of the cattle drives.

Right: An early photograph of a Montana cattle ranch. The cattle have been contained in pens.

Charles Goodnight

Below: Charles Goodnight made his fortune from the Texas Longhorn.

The greatest real-life cowboy of them all, Charles Goodnight was born in Macoupin County, Illinois in 1836, but his family trekked west in 1846, the so-called Year of Decision. He was to become the best-known cattle rancher ever, celebrated as the "father of the Texas Panhandle." Historian J. Frank Dobie wrote that Goodnight "approached greatness more nearly than any cowman of history." In 1856, Goodnight started work as a cowboy, but as war approached, he joined the Texas Rangers in 1857. Later, he fought with the Confederacy during the Civil War. When hostilities ceased, his first great cattle-driving enterprise was the famous "making the gather." During the war, thousands of cattle had roamed loose across the South. The gather was a round-up of the huge Texas Longhorn herd, which was then driven to the railroad heads. This task completed, Goodnight turned his hand to more conventional enterprise.

Charles Goodnight had a huge influence on the culture of the West, and is even credited with having coined the modern use of the term "cowboy." He had a close, almost paternal relationship with his men, and forbade them to drink, swear, or play cards. This inveterate plainsman was a cattle industry pioneer, who made a huge contribution to the hugely lucrative practice of driving cattle to market. He developed an economic and efficient method of droving that is still in use today.

Under his management, the drive usually started after breakfast and continued until a midday lunch. Towards evening, the trail boss would scout ahead for a safe place to bed down for the night. A herd of three-thousand cattle needed between twelve and fifteen drovers, including the trail boss, cook, and wrangler. The status of the cowboys themselves was determined by his place on the drive. The most important men were the lead riders, who guided the herd at the front. The outriders at the flanks were next in rank, followed by the drag riders at the back of the herd, who ate a lot of dust and comprised the bottom of the pecking order. Goodnight also instituted nighthawk watches, where two-man teams took turns guarding the herd, circling round the animals on horseback to keep them together. Although a herd usually moved at around ten to twelve miles a day, speeds of up to twenty-four miles a day could be achieved in good conditions by expert drovers.

Overleaf: A humorous evocation of life on the trail. Cookie runs from a stampeding cow that has overturned the coffee pot onto the camp fire.

Above: The King of the Cowboys, Charles Goodnight, was
born in 1836 and died in 1929. He was one of the first men
to see the financial potential of the cattle industry.

The Goodnight-Adair Partnership

The Goodnight-Adair partnership became one of the most successful associations of capital and ranching know-how in the West, and provided a pattern for many smaller enterprises.

John George Adair was born in Ireland in 1823. He was a Protestant of Scottish-Irish descent. Adair was an intelligent man who attended the prestigious Trinity College University in Dublin and trained to join the British Diplomatic Service, but ended up going into business instead. His family were Irish landowners, and Adair himself built the magnificent Glenveagh Castle in County Donegal, Ireland. Adair had soon realised the huge opportunities offered by western expansion, and he opened offices in both New York City and Denver, Colorado. In 1869, Adair married a well-connected American widow, Cornelia Wadsworth Ritchie.

Adair met his second-most-important partner, Charles Goodnight, in Denver in 1874, when both men were taking part in an organized buffalo hunt. Goodnight opened Adair's eyes to the fortunes that could be made from large-scale ranching, and persuaded Adair to invest in a massive ranch. The two partners were to sign two five-year-long partnership agreements. The J. A. Ranch (named for Adair's initials, at Goodnight's suggestion) was bought with Adair's capital, and Goodnight was to manage the concern at an annual salary of $2,500. The ranch was located in a beautiful area in the Palo Duro Canyon in the Texas Panhandle, and was liberally supplied with plenty of water, timber, game, and fantastic grazing land. At its height in 1883, the ranch covered 1,335,000 acres, and the partners owned over a hundred-thousand grazing cattle. Goodnight became an important Texas cattleman, and became a co-founder of the Panhandle Stockman's Association in 1880. The aim of the association was to improve cattle breeding and repel the threat of rustlers. Goodnight himself preserved a herd of native bison on his ranch, and crossed these with domestic cattle to produce the "cattalo."

Although Goodnight appreciated Adair's financial backing, he thoroughly disliked his hard-drinking, fiery-tempered personality. He was also frustrated by Adair's more conservative approach to land acquisition. Despite these differences, the partnership between the two men was extremely successful. By the end of their first five years together, the partners had made $510,000. In fact, Adair only visited the J. A. Ranch three times before he died in 1885, so Goodnight did not have to suffer too much of his company.

Adair was no more popular in his native Ireland, where he had cleared many families from his property to beautify the setting of Glenveagh Castle. On the night before his burial in Killenard, Ireland, the local people threw a dead dog into his open grave. Two years later, a lightning bolt shattered his memorial stone into a thousand pieces.

After Adair's death, his wife Cornelia took over the partnership with Goodnight, and they worked together until 1888. Things between them were not always smooth, as Cornelia was fairly opinionated about how her money should be spent. At this time, Goodnight decided to leave the partnership to buy his own slightly smaller concern. He bought the 140,000 acre Quitaque Ranch, where he grazed twenty thousand head of cattle. By this time, Goodnight had realised that the days of the lucrative open range were numbered, with the advent of the Fort Worth and Denver City Railroad, arable farming, and barbed wire-fenced enclosures.

Left: Cookie was a highly valued member of the trail team. The chuck wagon was a great help to him in his work.

The Chuck Wagon

Charles Goodnight first introduced the iconic chuck wagon in 1866. Texas rancher, cattle king, and co-founder of the famous Goodnight-Loving trail, Goodnight understood the huge importance that cowhands placed on "larrupin' good" victuals.

Overleaf: An early photograph of trailhands gathering around the chuck wagon for coffee. Note cookie working on the drop-down flap.

Above and opposite page: The chuck wagon was not only a work station, but was also a means of transporting food along the trail. Closed up, it could be drawn along by a horse or an ox.

The first chuck wagon was constructed from wood and drawn by oxen. The chuck box, sited towards the rear of the wagon, had a hinged lid that dropped down to become the food preparation area. The box also contained various drawers and compartments, which held the cooking equipment (Dutch ovens, skillets, and the all-important coffee pot) along with various easily-preserved staples such as cornmeal, flour, dry beans, jerky, dried fruit, molasses, coffee, sourdough starter, and chilli peppers. Often second only in importance to the trail boss, the chuck wagon "cookie" not only used the materials packed in the wagon, but also foraged for locally available game and produce. Chuck wagon cooks make brief appearances in many Westerns, and are often comedic characters. John Wayne's 1972 film The Cowboys, for example, features a chuck wagon chef named Jeb Nightlinger. On the ranch, Cookie usually slept in the cookhouse rather than the cowboy bunkhouse. Wagon cooks often enforced respect for their food stores with the edge of their skillets.

Unsurprisingly, meat was a large component of the grease-hungry cowboy diet. Although they had a ready supply of fresh beef, the trail diet was livened up with venison, wild turkey, squirrel, quail, duck, rabbit, and grouse. Cookie might also collect herbs (especially sage), acorns, buckwheat, nuts, greens, and wild berries along the trail. By the 1880s, some canned goods were available to chuck wagon cooks on the northern range, including tomatoes, peaches, and condensed milk. These luxuries had migrated to the southern range by the 1890s. But although authentic chuck wagon recipes sometimes include fresh dairy products and eggs, these were not in general use before the 1920s.

Cowboys often sought to work for the bosses with the best trail cooks, and even described their trail work as "riding the grub line." Western writers such as Louis L'Amour, were quick to celebrate the mythical powers of chuck wagon cooks to charm the least promising ingredients into appetizing meals. Retired cowboys who settled down to ranching missed not only the freedom of the trail, but chuck wagon coffee and biscuits cooked on an open fire. By the same token, unskilled cooks were reviled and heaped with unfriendly epithets, including belly cheater, grub worm, gut robber, and pot rustler.

While bunkhouse cooks had access to a greater range of equipment and foodstuffs, they could not rival the esteem accorded to a good cook on the open range. Trail bosses rewarded these men with better wages than those of the regular cowboys. While some cowboy dishes — like possum roast and rattlesnake soup — may have lost their appeal over the years, many chuck wagon recipes still sound mighty appetizing. Here are just a few of the most well known: cowboy sausages and sweet taters, Texas camp bread (the recipe dates from the 1850s), spotted pup dessert (mostly rice and raisins), chuck wagon beans, buffalo steaks with chipotle-coffee rub, chuck wagon stew, Missouri-style barbecued ribs, and Indian breakfast.

Opposite page: Chuck wagon coffee and camp bread were an essential part of the trail diet.

Left: Cookie used the chuck wagon to keep his condiments and cooking utensils safe and clean.

Another hugely important part of a cowboy's diet was coffee. Coffee was served from the chuck wagon throughout the day. An apocryphal coffee recipe instructs that two pounds of good strong coffee should be wetted down with a little water and boiled for two hours. A horseshoe should then be thrown into the mixture. If the horseshoe sank, the coffee should be boiled some more.

Below: A Dutch skillet was often stood on the camp fire embers to cook a nourishing stew.

The most famous brand of cowboy coffee was Arbuckle's. The Arbuckle Brothers of Pittsburgh, Pennsylvania produced pre-roasted coffee beans that became hugely popular in the Old West. Their recipe for good coffee was to throw a handful of their ground beans into a cup of water. Before the Civil War, coffee was sold green, and the beans had to be roasted in a skillet over the campfire before they could be used. A single burned bean could ruin a whole batch. John and Charles Arbuckle developed a patented method of roasting coffee beans and sealing in their flavor and aroma with an egg and sugar glaze. The coffee was then sold in patented airtight, one-pound packages. These bore their highly distinctive red, yellow, and black labels, which were printed with the Arbuckle name and their flying angel trademark. Many cowboys didn't even know that other types of coffee existed. Arbuckle's packages became synonymous with coffee on the trail, and were a huge and instant hit with chuck wagon cooks. Brilliant marketing men, the Arbuckle brothers also introduced collectible coupons into their packaging that could be redeemed for useful stuff like razors, neckerchiefs, and wedding rings. They also included a peppermint stick in each pack of coffee, which chuck wagon cooks often used as a reward for any cowboy who would agree to take over the coffee grinding duties.

Goodnight's innovative chuck wagon became one of the most iconic and useful pieces of Western equipment. Used on the cattle drives for decades, a modern form of the chuck wagon is still in use.

Cattlemen like Goodnight changed the fortunes of the whole region. Having made several fortunes and gone bust several times, he finally died at his ranch at the age of ninety-three. Rumor has it that he had survived for years on a diet of coffee, beef, and Cuban cigars.

The Texas Longhorn

Charles Goodnight and many other cattle barons made their fortune off the Texas Longhorn.

Texan stockmen created the breed by cross-breeding feral Mexican cattle and domesticated animals from the East. This resulted in tough, long-legged animals that required little water and could withstand blizzards, droughts, and dust storms. The toughness of the Longhorns meant that they lost very little weight along the cattle drive. The breed is best known for their towering horns, which can measure seven feet from tip to tip, and are used both for defense and attack. The Longhorn is also famous for its diverse coloring; their hides may be yellow, black, brown, red, or white. Although these beasts are known for their gentle and intelligent dispositions, they also have a highly developed survival instinct. They have an exceptionally strong sense of smell, which makes it easy for a cow to locate her own calf.

Longhorn bulls, on the other hand, are notoriously mean, and it takes very little provocation to turn one into a serious threat, both to other bulls and to humans. Only a very well-armed cowboy stood a chance against an angry Longhorn bull.

The Longhorn breed has retained its popularity over the years. In addition to their lean, low-cholesterol meat, the animals are prized today for their historic ties to the Old West. Longhorns are the official large mammal of Texas. The most expensive Longhorn ever was sold for $170,000.

Colt Lightning

SPECIFICATIONS

Caliber: Various ranging from.22 to .50-95

Barrel: 20, 22, 24, 26, and 28 inches

Type: Tubular magazine, slide-action rifle

Origin: Colt Armaments Manufacturing Co., Hartford, Connecticut

A medium-frame Lightning carbine with a twenty-inch barrel. The gun is in .44 caliber and has a saddle-ring

The Colt Lightning was designed by William Mason in 1877 and produced by the company between 1877 and 1909.

The Colt Lightning Magazine Rifle was first introduced in 1884. It was the first slide-action rifle to be manufactured by Colt. Based on two master patents registered to W. H. Elliott in 1883, the weapon was produced in three frame sizes. The small-frame version was available only in .22 caliber, while the medium- and large-frame versions were produced as both long-barrel rifles and short-barrel carbines. In addition, a special version of the medium-frame version was produced for the San Francisco Police department. The largest round for the large-frame rifle was the .50-95 Express. This gun earned the nickname Express model for all of its caliber versions. The Lightning was marketed by Colt as the rifle companion to the 1873 Colt Single-Action and the 1878 Double-Action revolvers. The operation of the action with the left hand or off hand was considered a positive improvement on the lever-action rifle. The magazine held either twelve or fifteen rounds depending on caliber. The Lightning Magazine Rifle would sell nearly 200,000 pieces before the model was retired in 1904.

Many examples of this handy weapon found their way out West.

A large-frame Lightning, chambered for a .40-60 cartridge. The gun has a twenty-eight-inch barrel.

The End of the Trails

The heyday of the cattle drives and the trails they used was between 1866 and 1890. Originally, the drives were a major stimulant to the burgeoning railroad network, but as the railroad tracks extended into previously uncharted territory, the need for long and dangerous cattle drives was gradually diminished. They were virtually obsolete by the 1890s. The advent of refrigerated railroad cars in the 1880s meant that, by the end of the century, fresh beef could be transported all the way to Europe by train and ship.

A combination of railroad expansion, the introduction of barbed wire-fenced pastures, and irrigation windmills gradually tamed huge stretches of the Western plains. Barbed wire was invented by Illinois farmer Joseph Farwell Glidden, and patented by him in 1874. This was a cheap and portable fencing material made from twisted wire with spaced coiled barbs. It was used to segment the open prairies of the West into enclosed grazing land and made a huge impact on the society and economy of the region. Ranchers could now isolate their cattle and control breeding. Although the material can cause hide injuries to livestock, it is still widely used today. It was barbed wire that finally closed down the Chisholm Trail in 1884, and drastically reduced the open routes available to the Western trails.

Below: Glidden used a
coffee mill to form the first
barbs, which he attached
to a length of wire. His
invention changed Western
ranching forever.

The era of the trails had lasted for around twenty-five years and exerted a great influence on the life of the frontier.

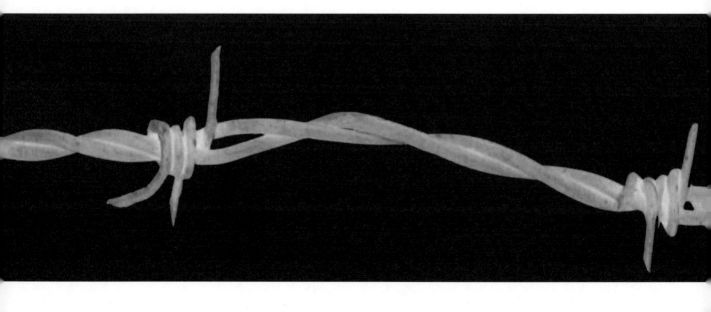

Right: Ranchers used Glidden's "devil's rope" to enclose thousands of acres. This effectively ended the days of the trails and the open range.

Above: William Edenborn refined Glidden's concept and invented a humane fence wire that did not harm cattle.

The End of the Open Range

The changes that Goodnight recognized resulted in a shift away from cattle grazing on the open range towards fenced-in ranching. Before it was enclosed, the open range was a huge area of public-domain land in the central and northern Great Plains. It sprawled across several states including Texas, Kansas, Montana, Nebraska, North Dakota, South Dakota, and Wyoming. The years of open-range cattle grazing were brief, thriving between around 1866 and 1890. This cow country was free from farmers, fencing, and grass-eating sheep, but it was not completely unmanaged. Where water was in short supply, wells were drilled and dams constructed. Windmills were also built to pump up underground water so that ranches did not need to be sited near a river or stream. Individual cattle herds were branded to show who owned them. This meant burning a specific logo onto the cow's hide with a hot iron rod, usually on the left hip. Branded cows could be separated into different herds at round-up time and driven to market.

For a couple of decades, open range grazing was hugely profitable, and attracted many investors from the United States and Europe. The government supported the cattle industry by banning fencing of the range lands, and awarding contracts to feed the reservation-bound Indians to cattle companies.

The end of the open range was hastened by the terrible conditions of 1886 and 1887. A toxic combination of desperate overgrazing of the prairie grasses by non-native species of cattle (by an estimated thirty-five to forty million animals) and atrocious weather conditions led to an ecological disaster. There was an extreme drought in the spring of 1886, followed by a scorching summer when temperatures on the prairie soared to 109 degrees Fahrenheit. The following January (1887), a tremendous winter storm hit the region, and temperatures fell to forty-three degrees below zero. A devastating famine ensued, and it is estimated that over half of the cattle on the prairie succumbed. Many cowboys also perished from cold and hunger. Effectively, the days of the wide-open spaces were numbered. Many cattle operations were bankrupted and investors ruined.

The need for private individuals to manage the land properly, rather than exploiting it, meant that ranching of enclosed acres became much more widespread. Publicly owned grazing land was gradually enclosed. Almost nothing of the open range remained by 1890.

This change in the way the prairie was managed was also helped by the

Left: Even barbed wire did not stop problems erupting between farmers and ranchers.

pacification of the Plains tribes. On the positive side, enclosure went some way to slow down the decimation of the wild buffalo. This more business-like approach to raising cattle also meant that ranches became sound financial investments for savvy entrepreneurs and their financial backers, like Charles Goodnight and his investor, John G. Adair. Huge fortunes were made, and it is estimated that by 1885, just thirty-five cattle barons owned one-and-a-half million cattle between them. About two-thirds of the western lands were now being used for grazing.

Not everyone was happy about the cattle ranchers' domination of this entire region. Writing in 1955, Bernard DeVoto wrote a damning description of this system. "The cattlemen came from Elsewhere into the empty West. They were always arrogant and always deluded... They kept sheepmen out of the West... [and] did their utmost to keep the nester, the farmer, the actual settler, the man who could create local and permanent wealth out of the West... the big cattlemen squeezed out the little ones wherever possible... frequently hiring gunmen to murder them."

The move to ranching also led to a changing focus for cowboys, who became more orientated towards animal husbandry than herding. Their new duties included feeding, branding, ear marking, and basic veterinary care. They were also responsible for maintaining the ranch-land, its water supply, and its boundaries.

The end of the cattle drives brought a gradual end to the male-dominated live of the West. Trail life slowly gave way to the more traditional family life of farmers and settlers. The frontier itself was declared ended in 1890, but thousands of square miles of the West remained unsettled for many years.

Overleaf: The winter storm of January 1887 became known as "the Great Die-Up" because it killed so many grazing animals. Many humans were also lost.

Remington Model 1890

The Remington New Model Army Revolver proved to be serious competition for Colt's output during the Civil War. Over 120,000 guns were delivered. As the Civil War came to an end, it became clear that the metallic cartridge had superseded the percussion system. The Rollin White patent of 1855 prevented other manufacturers from using bored-through cylinders until 1869 when the patent expired. Its expiration led to a rush of new revolver designs at the beginning of the 1870s, and many percussion conversions. First rimfire and then centerfire ammunition was used. The most successful of this generation of guns was the Colt Model 1873.

Remington's answer to the Colt model was its Model 1875 Outlaw, a heavy army-caliber revolver. Originally made for Remington's own .44 caliber centerfire cartridge, Model 1875s were then produced in .44-40 and .45 long Colt calibers. This cartridge revolver retained Remington's signature triangular web under the ejector rod. Whilst this feature was extolled as a

SPECIFICATIONS

Caliber: .44 and .45

Barrel: 7 and 5 inches

Type: Six shot, single-action cartridge revolver

Origin: Remington Armory, Ilion, New York

Remington Model 1875 Outlaw Revolver

SPECIFICATIONS

Caliber: .44-40 WCF

Barrel: 7 and 5 inches

Type: Six-shot, single-action cartridge revolver

Origin: Remington Armory, Ilion, New York

was just 25,000 units. The gun was used extensively in the West and its owners include outlaws like Frank James, a fact that probably contributed to its name.

positive virtue in barrel location and firing accuracy, it always imparted a clumsier outline to the Remington than that of the more attractive Colt.

The gun was finished in nickel plate or blued. Grips were in oiled walnut, mother of pearl and ivory. Although an effective weapon, the total production of the Model 1875 Outlaw

Remington is the oldest company in America that is still making its original product.

In 1888, E. Remington & Sons went bankrupt, and the company changed its name to Remington Arms. Before the arrival of the Model 1890, a few Model 1888s were produced, though officially there was no such model. Closely resembling the Colt Model 1873 Single Action Army, this shorter-barreled revolver finally removed the triangular web under the barrel. Available only in .44-40 caliber, the 1890 came with a five-inch barrel. Fewer than five-hundred examples were made between 1888 and 1889.

The official Model 1890 was manufactured between 1891 and 1894. Exactly two-thousand twenty examples were produced, making this a fairly unsuccessful gun. These days it is extremely collectible. Available with either five- or seven-inch round barrels (roll-stamped Remington Arms Co.) the gun came with a choice of hard rubber or ivory grips, and had a blued or nickel-plated finish. A lanyard ring was a popular factory-fitted accessory for this gun as shown on this example.

Cowboy Kit

A cowboy needs wide-open spaces.

A cowboy needs wild, untamed places

A cowboy needs untrammeled trails.

A cowboy needs grassy hills and dales.

Paul Harwitz, A Cowboy Needs

Above: Cowboy equipment is instantly recognizable.

One of the most recognizable aspects of the classic American cowboy was (and is) his classic outfit and equipment. The kit evolved over many years, with practicality as the ultimate goal. Many of its elements were derived from the original outfit of the Mexican vaqueros; aspects of this cowboy kit were adapted for the many different regions of the American West and the challenges posed by their climates and terrains.

Traditionally, the cowboy wore a wide-brimmed hat to protect his face from the sun, wind, rain, and snagging branches. The brim usually measured between four and six inches, and was inspired by the Spanish sombrero (which took its name from sombra, the Spanish word for "shade"). They were high-crowned to keep the head cool in hot weather. A "stampede string" under the chin kept the hat in place in windy weather and during rough riding. The "stampede string" was a long leather lace that ran half way round the crown of the hat then through a hole on each side; the ends were knotted under the chin or at the back of the head. The original cowboy hats were so regionally variable that it was said that you could tell where a cowhand came from just by the crease in his hat. The most

Above: The classic wide-brimmed cowboy hat was derived from the Mexican sombrero.

famous maker of cowboy headgear was John Batterson Stetson, a professional hatter who popularized a felted version used by generations of cowboys, the iconic "Boss of the Plains." The hat was so successful that Stetson built a large national corporation on its popularity. "The Boss of the Plains" was adopted by many famous westerners, including Buffalo Bill, Annie Oakley, Calamity Jane, and Will Rogers. The infamous ten gallon hat was created for Buffalo Bill Coady as an exaggerated stage prop for his Wild West Show. Stetson continued to make the model for particularly flamboyant cowboys. Contrary to the name, the hat was never able to hold ten gallons of anything.

Above: An early cowboy hat.

The properly-attired cowboy wore a bandana around his neck, which was also known as a wild rag, a mascada, or kerchief. An authentic wild rag was usually made from silk and was between thirty-six and forty-four inches square. The usually red fabric was folded into a triangle and tied at the back of the neck. Although it was often elaborately knotted, these ties had to release quickly

Above: The Boss of the Plains became the iconic headgear for cowboys.

Left: A low-crowned cowboy hat.

Right: The classic bandana was also known as a wild rag, mascada, or kerchief.

Right: The cowboy boots on the left have the traditional square toe. Those on the right are round-toed.

in dangerous situations to prevent the rider from being dragged by his scarf. The natural silk fabric of the bandana was chosen for practicality: it was warm in winter and could be used to mop the face or cover the mouth on the dusty summer trails. It could also be used as earmuffs in cold weather and to protect the eyes from snow blindness. In the summer, the cloth protected cowboys from deadly sunburn. The bandana might also be used to hold a hot pot or branding iron, or employed as a makeshift tourniquet or sling in case of injury.

Horsemen have always needed protective footwear, and have often preferred boots with a higher heel. Some early riding boots were based on the English Wellington, a plain leather boot with one-inch heels and straight tops. Cowboys wore high-topped boots to protect his lower leg from chafing during long hours in the saddle. Originally, cowboy boots had square or rounded toes (cowboy boots with pointed toes did not become the standard until the 1950s). These narrower toes helped the cowboy to get his feet in the stirrups, and their high heels kept them from slipping through them. The heels also provided a brace when the cowhands were roping. The boot soles were usually made from slick, smooth leather to stop them catching when dismounting, but they also wore hessian boots. The famous Coffeyville-style cowboy boot was first made in Coffeyville, Kansas around 1870. These boots were usually made from smooth black leather and equipped with a low Cuban heel. The front of the boot (the "graft") was made higher than the back of the boot, and was often in a contrasting color. Texan cowboys often had a Lone Star motif inlaid in the boot. With the prevalence of cowboy radio shows in the 1920s and '30s, cowboy boots became fashion items, with their design becoming more colorful and intricate in the 1940s and '50s. When line-dancing became popular in the 1990s, rhinestone and precious stone inlays became popular. Cowboy boots continue to be highly popular.

Many working cowboys fitted their boots with spurs (la espuela). Spurs are u-shaped devices attached to the heel of the boot by the spur strap; a small metal neck or "shank" sticking out of the spurs is used to poke the horse's sides as a means of steering. Spurs were used to give tired legs a stronger action. Western spurs were often made from metal, and often had a small, serrated wheel attached

Left: Cowboys used spurs to give their tired legs stronger action.

at the end of the spur's shaft. Known as the rowel (or la rodaja or la estrella in Spanish), the wheel or star turned as the rider's heel touched the horse's side. Jingle bobs were also attached to the rowel. These were partly decorative and made a bell-like ringing sound when the spurs moved. They supposedly kept the cowboy's horse alert. Cowboy boots were adapted for each different region, and special boots were made for certain jobs. Roper boots with flat heels were used for working in arenas and for walking, while laced packer boots were made from heavy leather for cold weather hiking and really hard riding.

Above: Many cowboy spurs were equipped with a rowel, or star, that turned as the heel touched the horse.

Right: Levi Strauss was born in Bavaria, Germany, in 1829. He sailed to New York at age eighteen. In January 1853, Strauss became an American citizen, sailing to the West that March.

Left and below: Winters on the trail could be just as cold as the summers were hot, so a cowboy needed a selection of weather gear.

Most cowboys wore sturdy denim jeans to prevent tangling with brush or equipment, and were among the first groups of Americans to popularize this practical garment. Levi Strauss opened his eponymous company in San Francisco in 1853, and gained the patent for his famous reinforcing rivet in 1873. The inside leg seams of cowboy jeans were rolled so that they wouldn't rub his legs when he was on horseback. Cowboys often rolled their Levis up at the bottom in the traditional "four-horse roll" cuff. It was said that polite cowboys used the four-inch turn-ups for their cigarette ash when ashtrays were hard to find.

Further protection for the legs against weather and brush was offered by chaps (correctly pronounced as "shaps"). These were a highly important part of the cowboy rig that were worn over jeans. The terms were derived from the Spanish las

Right: Cowboys wearing various styles of chaps.

Below: A pair of angora chaps, or "woolies." The leather batwing chaps have been embellished with decorative leather patches.

chaparreras, or chaparejos. They were based on the armas of early Spanish and Mexican riders who wore them when they were herding cattle. Essentially, these were two large pieces of cowhide attached to the horn of the rider's saddle stock. These apron-style chaps gradually evolved into the more elaborate versions worn by the American cowboy, which were closer to the leather leggings worn by the Indians. Chaps came in many different styles and varieties, each tailored for the local conditions. Shotgun chaps, for example were tight fitting garments that could be worn as trousers. They had no snaps or rings but often had full length zippers. By contrast, batwings were long chaps with big leather flaps, fastened with rings and snaps. These were often worn by rodeo cowboys. Angora chaps or "woolies" were covered with long Angora goat hair and were usually lined with canvas. They were used as protection against the cold in Wyoming and Montana and the open prairie country. They appeared on the Great Plains in the late 1880s. Chinks were short chaps, or leather riding aprons, and were often fringed. They were favored by cowboys in Texas and the southwest. They sometimes wore chinks with their pants tucked into high boots. Texan cowboys also wore shotgun chaps or stovepipes. These were straight, narrow

leggings, popular in the 1870s. Better at trapping body heat, they were especially useful in cold and windy weather. In the summer, Texan cowboys often preferred batwing chaps. These were cut wide, with a flare at the bottom. Usually made from smooth leather, they allowed for greater air circulation than stovepipes, making them much cooler. Armitas were a Californian version of chinks made by hand. When wearing chaps, cowboys often wore chap guards on their spurs to prevent them from fouling the rowel.

On their hands cowboys wore thick hide gloves, sometimes decorated with long leather fringes. They might also use leather wrist cuffs for protection against brush and branches, to prevent wear to their shirtsleeves, or to stop a rope from fouling. Leather jackets were also popular with men riding the trail and might also be decorated with long fringes. For bad weather, there was the pommel slicker, a long

Above: These leather gloves have the classic leather cuffs and fringing favored by cowboys.

Left: A diverse mix of cowboys wearing a wide selection of gear. Almost all wear a hat and kerchief.

Above: A braided leather cowboy whip, mostly used for its cracking sound, which could drive or direct herds as needed.

Below: Various lasso nooses used for catching cattle.

waterproof coat designed to protect the rider and his saddle from rain and snow.

Every working cowboy also carried a modest selection of equipment. These were often packed into his so-called "war bag" (or "possibles bag"). These typically contained a spare set of clothes, ammunition, playing cards, the bill of sale for the cowby's horse, his makins (see section Cowboy Lingo), and personal effects like a harmonica some precious letters from home. On the trail, a cowboy would also carry a bedroll. This was a roll of blankets or comforters for sleeping in, and was also called a "dreaming sack", "sugan", "soogan", or "hot roll." In bad weather, a cowboy might also pack a teepee or small canvas tent to take shelter in. These became popular from the 1880s onwards and are still in use today. They are sometimes called range teepees or teepee tents. A cowboy was also likely to carry a quart (from the Spanish word la cuarta). This was a short leather strap or braided whip, which often had a handle attached to it, used to increase a horse's speed. A loop was usually attached to the handle so that a rider could wear it around his wrist, or hang it over the saddle horn.

Because of the nature of a cowboy's work, ropes of various lengths and materials were a very important aspect of his kit. A lariat or lasso (Spanish el lazo) was made from braided rawhide or hemp. A hondo, or loop, was attached to one end, and the other end was passed through this. This kind of rope was also known as a "lash rope", "string", or "catch rope". When made from braided hide, the lasso was known as a reata, "riata", or "skin-string". Different hides made ropes of a different texture and stiffness. Bull hide, for example, made a very stiff rope, used for heel roping. Mexican cowboys kept their reatas supple by tying them between two trees and rubbing them first with lemon juice and then with beef fat (suet). Reatas could be very long indeed, up to eighty feet or more. A rope made from plant fiber (such as Manila hemp, sisal, or cotton) is called a sogo. The term in taken from the

Spanish la soga, from which our word, "lasso," is also derived. Other ropes were also popular in cowboy country. Maguey is a Mexican style rope made from agave fiber. "Pigging strings," as they were known in the Great Basin, were short lengths of rope that cowboys carried in their chaps or on their saddles. This kind of rope was pretty much universal, though known by many different terms, including "hoggin' string" in Texas, a "tie-down rope" in the Southwest, and a "short line" in British Columbia, Canada. A cowboy often mounted a useful catch rope on his saddle, attached by a leather rope strap. Standard cowboy roping maneuvers included the backhand flip, forefooting, heeling, the pitch, and the hoolihan. Many cowboys also carried a metal marlin spike for punching holes and unlacing leather, among many other uses.

Although every cowboy aspired to own an expensive pistol, they were more likely to carry old Civil War guns, like the Spencer Repeating Rifle. The ultimate cowboy weapon was Winchester's 1866 Carbine. This more sophisticated weapon used rimfire cartridges, and its relatively compact barrel (twenty inches) made it

Above: A cowboy poses with his carefully coiled rope. He probably sent copies of this studio photograph to friends and family back home.

Colt Model 1877 Thunderer

Western outlaw John Wesley Hardin used both the "Lightning"
and "Thunderer" versions of the Model 1877.

The Model 1877 D.A. was Colt's first foray into the field of double-action pistols. It appeared three years before Smith & Wesson produced their first double-action gun. Originally called the New Double-Action Self-Cocking Central Fire Six-Shot Revolver, the Model 1877 was designed by Colt's well-known employee, William Mason. Mason also designed the famed Single-Action Army Model of 1873. The double action gave the Thunderer a much faster rate of fire. Gunfighters and cowboys alike loved the gun for this reason.

At first sight the gun looks a lot like the famous Peacemaker, except for its signal rear-offset "birds head" grip. The grip was made from either hard rubber or walnut and gave the gun its very distinctive look. The frame is somewhat smaller than that of the Single-Action, and the section of frame in front of the trigger is cut away slightly. Many cowboy cap pistols from the 1930s were modeled on this gun. In use, the Model 1877's action proved over-complicated and hard to repair. Despite this, some 166,000 examples were made between 1877 and 1909. It is not recommended to fire original examples today.

This version of the Thunderer was chambered for .41 Colt ammunition. It came in two barrel lengths, three-and-a-half and four-and-a-half-inches. The nickel finish is in beautiful condition; the gun is unlikely to have been used on the trail for too long.

SPECIFICATIONS

Caliber: .41 Colt

Barrel: 3½ inches

Type: Double-action centerfire revolver

Origin: Colt PFA Mfg Co., Hartford, Connecticut

A third version of the gun, known as the "Rainmaker," was also launched in 1877.

easy to stow in a saddle scabbard. With no bolt action, it was quick to draw and fire straight from the saddle. Larger-barreled guns, like the Henry Rifle, were also highly regarded on the plains. As well as warding off trouble, cowboys used their weapons to control varmints and shoot game. Heavier rifles, like the Sharps and Spencers, were usually used for larger targets like buffalo.

Knives were also an intrinsic part of every part of cowboy's equipment, and many carried the famous Bowie knife. Jim Bowie originated his unique curved steel blade in the very earliest years of the nineteenth century. Born in Kentucky in 1796, James Bowie was a prominent frontiersman who fought in the Texas Revolution, dying at the Battle of the Alamo in 1836. During his short but active life, Bowie became notorious for his ability as a knife fighter and was credited with designing the knife that bears his name. But in a letter to The Planter's

Right: These riveted leather cuffs show how cowboys preferred decorative gear.

Opposite page: This casual cowboy wears his holster in the cross-body draw position.

Left, above, and below: There is now a thriving market for Western cowboy memorabilia.

Above: The Hermann H. Heiser Saddlery Company of Denver, Colorado, was renowned for its leather gun belts, holsters, saddles, and tack.

Above: The heavily tooled leather of this gun belt and matching holsters demonstrates how cowboys spent their pay.

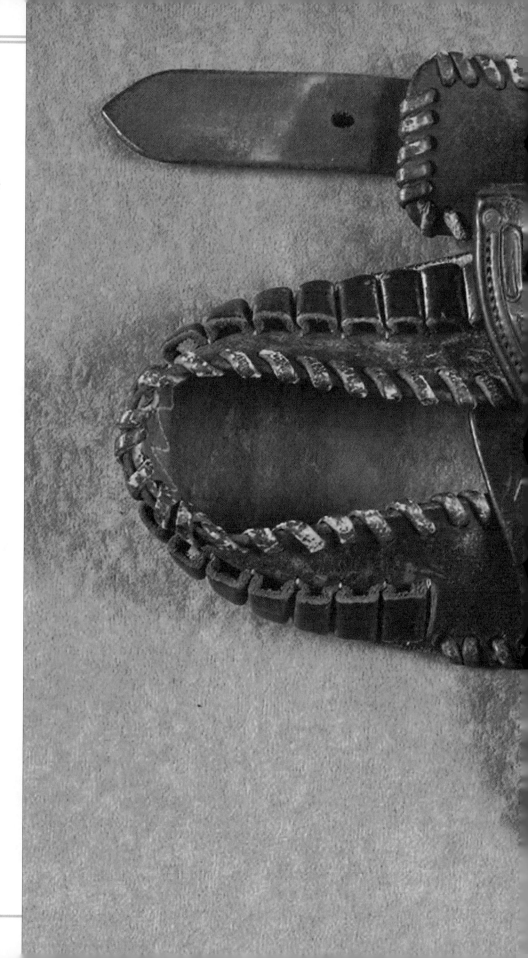

Right: A Buscadero fancy holster rig designed for a pair of Colt Peacemakers. Despite its deep decorative tooling, the main purpose of this holster is a speedy draw. There is nothing to impede the rapid removal of the gun it holds.

Fancy holsters were
made all over the
West, including Texas
and Colorado.

Colt Model 1872

Colt patented their centerfire revolver
cartridge in 1871. They developed it for use
by the United States Army.

This weapon is a prime example of how even a major manufacturer renowned for its innovation can get things horribly wrong. The U.S. Army had already decided that its future handguns would have a solid frame (i.e. they would have a top strap). It was clear that for both the military and civilian markets the future lay with the centerfire cartridge. Despite this, Colt produced a weapon without a top strap that was chambered for the .44 rimfire round. It was produced with five, seven, and eight-inch barrels, and had a smooth-sided cylinder chambered for six rounds. The gun was engraved with a naval scene. The overall design is reminiscent of the earlier generation of Colt weapons that were widely used during the Civil War, such as the 1860 army model. Seven-thousand examples of the Model 1872 were manufactured between 1871 and 1872. By Colt standards, the gun was a failure. The Model 1872's main significance is that it was Colt's first original design for a metallic round, as opposed to a conversion. The gun paved the way for the Single-Action Colt Army of 1873. Due to the low production figure, well-preserved examples of the Model 1872 are hard to find. Many of the original guns went to the American frontier where they were hard-used.

The cartridge remained in Colt production until the 1940s.

SPECIFICATIONS

Caliber: .44 rimfire

Barrel: 5, 6, 7 and 8 inches

Type: Single-action rimfire, open-top revolver

Origin: Colt PFA Mfg Co., Hartford, Connecticut

Right: Cowboy horses were bred to be small and light and to have good "cow sense."

Opposite page: The traditional Western saddle has a deep seat and high pommel to keep sleepy cowboys from falling out of it.

Advocate, James's brother Rezin Bowie maintained that he had designed the blade. In either case, the Bowie knife was designed to be a combination tool and weapon, for use when camping, hunting, fishing, and fighting. James Bowie himself used an early version to win his famous Sandbar Fight of 1827. Over the years, many versions of the unique blade were developed. These varied from six to twelve inches long and one-and-a-half to two inches wide, but retained the overall design of the broad blade that tapered to a wicked curved point.

Perhaps the most important relationship in any cowboy's life was with his horse (caviada or caballa in Spanish). Cowboy horses used a variety of special tack and saddles, designed to be practical and comfortable to men who often spent all day in the saddle. The traditional Western saddle (la silla) had a deep secure seat with a high pommel (la teja) and cantle, and was equipped with wide stirrups, hanging from stirrup leathers. Many had a horn (la cabezal). This was a projection (often bent forward) above the pommel, where a cowboy might stow his rope, or dally it (wrap it counter-clockwise to hold the animal or object he had roped). Californian slick horns were left deliberately uncovered by any material (such as rubber or leather) so that the rope would slide rather than grab. This is thought to be gentler for both horse and cattle. Some Western saddles also had more than one cinch (or girth) to keep them stable, and might have a night latch, or safety strap, for the

rider to hang onto. Padded bucking rolls were also sometimes attached to the front of the saddle to help the rider stay put if he became tired or distracted. Keepers or leather ties were also attached to many saddles to secure loose equipment. The comfort of the horse was also considered. The saddle was made with a wide saddletree that distributed the rider's weight over a greater area of the horse's back, and a woolen horse blanket or pad would be placed under the saddle to prevent it chafing and rubbing. It also kept the saddle clean. These horse blankets were often woven by Native Americans or imported from Mexico. They were known as el cojin or el bastes in Spanish. Saddle bags, or las cantinas, were made from canvas or leather and placed over the rear extensions of the saddle to carry extra gear. At first Western women rode side-saddle, but when they needed to do real ranch work they began to ride astride.

Above: The metal rings on this saddle were used to secure a cowboy's equipment.

Stirrups varied widely from area to area and from job to job. Oxbow stirrups were particularly thin straps of metal or leather, and preferred by bronco riders. Bell stirrups were much wider and comfortable for longer rides across the big country. Cowboy stirrups were often fitted with tapaderos, or taps. These were stirrup covers designed to protect the rider's feet from brush and the weather. They were available in different styles to accommodate local conditions, including eagle bill, bulldog, and monkey nose.

At the business end of the horse, the Western bridle is usually equipped with a curb bit and has long split reins to give the rider as much control as possible. Bits are metal mouthpieces used to steer the horse. A great many variations were available, with different shapes and degrees of severity. These include half-breed, spade, snaffle, curb, and ring bits.

Western horse tack seems infinitely variable, with many different adaptations for regional conditions, but perhaps the most bizarre example are the snowshoes that Sierra horses used to wear in winter. These prevented horses from "post holing" in the snow. Young horses quickly learned the strange gait needed to

Above: Comfortable
soft leather stirrups.

Right: Saddle styles
varied from region to
region.

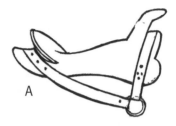

A

B

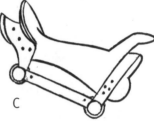

C

Right: This saddle used
long leather ties to secure
the cowboy's kit.

accommodate the shoes, but even older animals could be
trained to use them safely. Invented in Plumas County,
California, around 1866, horse snowshoes were sometimes
worn by horses pulling sleighs.

The horses themselves were specialized, too. Cowboy
horses were bred to be small and light, and to have good
"cow sense." Essentially, this meant knowing how to control
moving cattle. Many cowboy mounts were wild mustangs

Above: Saddle bags or *cantinas* were made from either leather or canvas. A cowboy used them to carry his personal gear.

and broncos descended from Arabian horses left behind by the Spanish explorers in the sixteenth century. They had completely adapted themselves to the Western habitat, and when they were captured and tamed they were highly valued for their endurance and intelligence. Quarter horses were also popular with trail-riding cowboys. They were the first all-American horse breed, and became the iconic mount of the West. In the nineteenth century, other famous breeds — like the Tennessee Walker, the Morgan, the Chickasaw, the Virginia Quarter-Miler, and the Paint —were selectively bred to ensure their suitability for the cattle drives.

Left: A Mexican saddle blanket. These were used to stop the saddle from chafing the horse and to keep the saddle itself clean.

Cowboy Working Conditions

Right and below: Branding was used from the early days of ranching. The iron brands were heated in a fire.

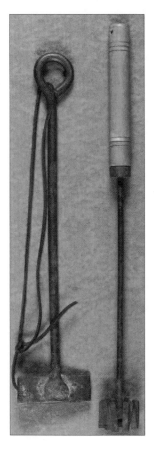

On the trail, a boss could earn around $125 a month, but an ordinary cowboy would be lucky to clear $40. $25 was more usual. Although food and coffee would be provided, the working hand had to supply his own clothes and equipment. This almost always meant that he also had to provide his own mount. Cowboys on the trail worked extremely long days of up to fourteen hours, and were used to sleeping for just six hours a night.

Ranch-based cowboys and cowboys in between trails usually lived together in communal bunkhouses. Also known as the "doghouse", "dive", "shack", "dump", "dicehouse", or "ram pasture", this was usually a barrack-like building with a single large, open room that was used for eating, sleeping, relaxing, and entertainment. When nature called, the cowboys used an outhouse. Indoors, each man had a narrow bed or cot and very little privacy. The bunkhouse was usually heated with a single wood stove.

Even today, ranches beyond the reach of a daily commute often provide bunkhouses for their staff. But these are comparatively luxurious, with electricity, heating, and indoor plumbing.

Right: Prairie weather conditions could be very challenging, even for Longhorns.

Right: This simple cowboy bunkhouse would be a very welcome sight on the prairie in mid-winter. A wood-burning stove was used to heat the room and to cook.

Cowboy Lingo

Opposite page: A cowboy tries to deflect stampeding cattle by waving his saddle blanket. His horse looks alarmed.

Acorn calf: an under-sized, sickly calf

Air the paunch: to vomit

Airing the lungs: cursing

Canned cow: canned milk

Cowpuncher: a long pole used to push the cattle into rail cars, also applied as another name for cowboys

Die-up: widespread destruction of cattle, usually the result of a natural disaster like a blizzard or drought

Greenhorn: a derogatory term for an Easterner unschooled in the ways of the West

Horse wrangler: an inexperienced cowboy who took care of the horses

Judas steer: an obedient steer used to quietly lead the other cattle to slaughter

Little Mary cowboy: the driver of the calf wagon, which was used to transport newborn calves

Mail order cowboy: a derogatory term meaning an immaculate, urban cowboy

Makins: the cigarette papers and tobacco used to roll cowboy cigarettes

Night Hawk: the unlucky cowboy chosen to stay awake at night to guard the saddles

Tenderfoot: an inexperienced cowhand

Ethnicity of the Cowboys

Opposite page: Western cowboys came from a range of ethnic backgrounds. Liberated slaves were attracted to the freedom of the open range.

Although the most popular image of the western cowboy is of a young white man from Texas or the Southeast, this does not reflect the varied backgrounds of the men who rode the trail. After the Civil War, many soldiers from both sides of the conflict rode west to start new lives or returned to their former lives on the range. The war also had an impact on the ethnic composition of the profession.

Some newly-freed black Americans were attracted to the freedom of riding the range and the relative lack of racial discrimination in the West. Many former Buffalo Soldiers also became cowboys, putting their riding skills to good use. As many as five-thousand men (or one-quarter of the men riding the line in Texas) were African-Americans. In fact, many of the most famous cowboys were black. These men included George Glenn (who rode the Chisholm Trail in 1870), Charlie Willis (the "Singing Cowboy"), and John Ware (the highly respected rancher).

It was a black cowboy, Texas Bill Pickett, who introduced steer wrestling to the sport of rodeo. Pickett was born on December 5, 1870 in Taylor, Texas, the thirteenth child of a former slave. He was to become known as the greatest cowboys of his day. Not lacking in courage, Pickett developed a technique of wrestling steers to the ground. His technique involved biting the sensitive lip of the animal. He subsequently adopted the stunt name of the "Bulldogger." In 1921, Pickett went on to star in two western movies, The Bull Dogger and The Crimson Skull. He died in 1932 after being kicked in the head by a wild bronco.

Nat Love was another famous African-American cowboy. Love was born in 1854, in Davidson County, Tennessee. His father was a slave foreman, and Nat himself was born a slave. Sadly, his father survived for only two years following his emancipation. Soon after his father's death, Love won a horse in a raffle, which he promptly sold. Sharing the money with his widowed mother, Love used his share to make his way to Dodge City, Kansas, to find work as a cowboy. He was hired as a hand on the Duval Ranch in Texas, and became one of the most admired cowboys in the West. Known as an expert horseman, roper, Indian fighter, marksman, and bronco rider, Love became known by the soubriquet of "Deadwood Dick". Love's

Below: Around a third of cowboys were from Mexico.

Above: Fifteen percent of Western cowboys were African-Americans.

personal motto reflected his considered outlook on life: "Every time you shoot at someone, plan on dying."

In the years after the Civil War, many Native Americans also became cowboys. Good men were in short supply at this time, and many hands were required to manage the massive cattle drives from Texas to the West. Native Americans were ideally equipped for this work, being experienced horsemen and accustomed to driving herds of buffalo and deer. Faced with depleted buffalo herds, many Indians had been forced to find an alternative way of life, with some becoming cowboys and ranchers. Men from several Indian tribes took up this line of work, including the Creeks, Seminoles, and Timucuas.

The Mexican cowboy tradition stretches right back to the Spanish conquistadors, who introduced horses and cattle to America. The men who herded these animals were the first vaqueros, or Mexican cowboys. They developed their skills of roping, branding, bronco riding, and rounding up cattle. Today, these skills are showcased in charreadas, a special kind of Mexican rodeo where the charros (Mexican cowboys) entertain the public. The original charreadas were held in the Mexican state of Jalisco, and were highly influential on the early rodeo competitions.

By the 1890s, it is estimated that an average of fifteen percent of cowboys were of African-American origin, around a third were from Mexico, and a fifth were Native Americans. If these figures are accurate, then as few as three in ten cowboys would have been white.

Regardless of their racial backgrounds, most cow-hands came from the poorer social classes. Cowboy life was always hard, often dangerous, and the pay was meager. On top of this, the profession carried a lowly social status. Their melancholy permeated the rich cowhand culture, whose songs and poems have been passed down to us.

Opposite page: This cowboy is a Native American from the Paiute tribe.

Winchester Model 1885

This is a standard Winchester High Wall Model 1885 sporting rifle. It has a thirty-inch .38-55 caliber barrel. Notice how the frame angles sharply upward, leaving the tip of the hammer spur visible.

SPECIFICATIONS

Caliber: .45 centerfire, .14 rimfire

Type: Single–shot rifle

Origin: Winchester Repeating Arms Co., New Haven, Connecticut

Oliver Winchester and several other shareholders created the Volcanic Repeating Arms Company in 1855. After the Civil War, he re-named it the Winchester Repeating Arms Company.

Life on the trail was dangerous, and a cowboy needed a rifle both for self-defense and for hunting. Winchester weapons were a popular choice in the West; their guns had a great reputation for being rugged and hardworking. Being mass-produced also meant that they offered good value for their cost. During the 1880s, single-shot rifles became more popular. Compared to repeating rifles, they are less wasteful of ammunition, easier to maintain, and more accurate.

The Winchester Model 1885 is a single-shot rifle with a falling block action designed by John M. Browning. Two popular models of the gun were produced. The Low Wall version showed an exposed hammer and fired less powerful cartridges. The High Wall used stronger cartridges. Its steel frame covered most of the firing hammer when viewed from the side. Officially, both guns were marketed by Winchester as the Single-Shot Rifle. The Model 1885 was offered with an extensive choice of calibers (including .45 centerfire and .14 rimfire types) as well as a wide variety of barrel lengths. These were either round or octagonal to match the caliber. Finishes and extras were available at additional cost.

The frame of this gun slants more gently forward and upward, at the
same angle as the top of the wrist. As the hammer and breech are visible,
we know that this is the Low Wall version of the Model 1885.

The Cowboy Code and Culture

Below: This cheerful band of cowboys appears to be hurrahing the town.

The most crucial "equipment" that every cowboy needed was strength of mind and body. The unspoken cowboy code of loyalty, honesty, common sense, and toughness came to be highly regarded. A true cowboy spoke little, but meant what he said; he was a strong man who chose to be gentle. These cowboy virtues have been embodied in many fictional characters, on the page and on screen, and remain powerful today. The cowboy code was a blend of Victorian and frontier values, and even retained a nod to the chivalric code of the Middle Ages. Their hazardous work and tough living conditions in isolated areas bred a tradition of self-dependence and individualism. A high value was placed on personal honesty.

1.   Never pass anyone on the trail without saying, "Howdy."

2.   When you leave town after a weekend of celebration, it is perfectly acceptable to shoot your pistols in the air and whoop like crazy. This is known as hurrahing a town.

3. When approaching a cowboy from behind, give a loud greeting before getting within pistol shot range.

4. Don't wave at a man on a horse. It may spook the animal. A nod of the head is the proper greeting.

5. After you pass someone on the trail, don't look back at him. This implies mistrust.

6. Riding another man's horse without his permission is completely unacceptable.

7. Never shoot an unarmed man. Don't shoot women at all.

8. A cowboy is pleasant even when out of sorts. Complaining is for quitters, and cowboys hate quitters.

9. Always be courageous. Cowboys hate cowards.

10. A cowboy always helps those in need, even strangers and enemies.

11. A horse thief may be hung without trial.

12. Never try on another man's hat.

13. Never shake a man awake. He may shoot you.

Above: This wide-eyed cowboy is saving his breath for breathing.

14. Real cowboys are modest. Braggarts are not tolerated.

15. A cowboy doesn't talk much. He saves his breath for breathing.

16. No matter how hungry and weary he is after a day in the saddle, a cowboy tends to his horse's needs first.

17. Curse all you want, but only around men, horses, and cows.

Although cowboy wages were low (an average of a dollar a day, plus food) the lifestyle attracted men from many different backgrounds and ethnicities as the cattle industry expanded.

Cowboy music dates from the heyday of the trail drives and cow camps, and are full of nostalgia, raw sentiment, death, fighting, and humor. The song titles are deeply evocative, and many form a part of country music culture to this day These songs include "The Texas Cowboy," "Blood on the Saddle," "The Old Cow Man,"

Above: These cowboys have removed their spurs and made themselves comfortable.

Opposite page: Cowboys taking a well-earned break by the river.

"The Streets of Laredo," "The Call of the Plains," and "The Drunken Desperado." These assorted cowboy verses carry some hint at the different emotions carried by the songs: wistful, tragic, and funny in turns.

It is also true that trail cowboys sang to the cattle at night. Songs like "Old Dan Tucker," "In the Sweet By and By," and "The Texas Lullaby" soothed jittery cows and reduced the likelihood of dangerous stampedes. Stampedes (the word comes from the Spanish estampida) were one of the most serious problems to beset cattle trails. Longhorn cattle were well-known to be more nervous than domesticated cattle, especially when being driven across unknown territory. Thunder and lightning were one of the most common causes of stampedes. If the cattle started running, cowboys were expected to jump into the saddle and try to head them off. This was an extremely dangerous job in the dark, so a full night of singing and patrolling the herd was worth the effort, if it meant avoiding a stampede. The job was usually

Opposite page: Cowboys bedded down near the smoldering embers of cookie's fire, next to the chuck wagon.

undertaken by two men, who circled around the herd on horseback at a walking pace, taking it in turns to sing verses of their cowboy melodies.

I'm wild and woolly and full of fleas,
I'm hard to curry below the knees,
I'm a she-wolf from Shannon Creek,
For I was dropped from a lightening streak
And it's my night to holler — Whoo-pee!
– from "The Drunken Desperado"

There was blood on the Saddle, blood all around
And a great big puddle of blood on the ground
The cowboy lay in it, all covered with gore
Oh pity the cowboy, all bloody and dead
A bronco fell on him and mashed his head.
– from "Blood on the Saddle"

Ho! Wind on the far, far prairies!
Free as the waves of the sea! Your voice is sweet as in alien street
The cry of a friend to me!
You bring me the breath of the prairies
Known in the days that are sped,
The wild geese's cry and the blue, blue sky
And the sailing clouds o'er head.
– from "The Call of the Plains"

Guitar playing was also popular among cowboys out on the range and in the bunkhouse. It was said that cowboys from Mexico and Spain first established the tradition. Guitars were ideal instruments for mobile cowboys, being inexpensive and small enough to fit into saddle bags. The image of cowboys strumming their instruments in the flickering light of the campfire is surely one of the most iconic. Over the years, cowboy guitarists developed their own style of playing, a hybrid of folk and country music with its own distinctive chords.

The famous guitar manufacturer Martin and Company has produced a range of guitars to honor the tradition of cowboy players. They launched the first guitar in

the series, the Cowboy X, in 2000, decorated with a painting of a traditional campfire scene by the Western artist Robert Armstrong. The model shown is a 2002 model, the Martin Cowboy III, which is decorated with an Armstrong painting of a typical ranch scene, complete with ranch hands, a cowgirl, and a bucking bronco.

Cowboy music is not the only art that celebrates the romance of trail life. Beginning in the 1880s, Wild West stage shows also enshrined and perpetuated the cowboy legend.

The Wild West Shows

Opposite page: Buffalo Bill Cody understood the appeal of cowboy skills.

The cowboy legend of the Old West was first commercially marketed by the "Wild West" shows of the day, including Buffalo Bill Cody's *Wild West Show*, which ran between 1884 and 1906. These shows were the first form of entertainment to take their inspiration from the lives and skills of the cowboys. Cody's show celebrated the most skillful and entertaining aspects of a cowhand's work, together with other aspects of the traditional West. Among his vignettes of Western life, Cody's show included a staged battle between cowboys and Indians. In fact, this is historically inaccurate; although cowboys would defend their cattle from rustlers of any ethnicity, most armed confrontation took place between the United States Cavalry and Native Americans. Cody's entertainment also included an

Below: Cody's famous show ran for more than twenty years.

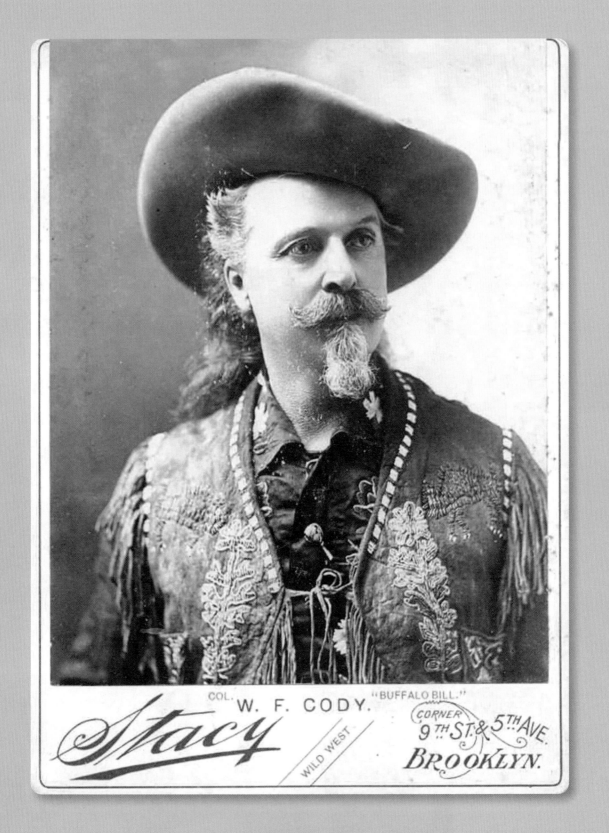

Right: Buffalo Bill surrounded by the cast of his show. The photograph shows an interesting blend of real cowboys and real Indians.

Opposite page: Cody was a master showman and knew exactly how to promote himself.

on-stage buffalo hunt, and an attack on the Deadwood stagecoach. The show also featured real-life Western characters such as Sitting Bull, Wild Bill Hickok, and Annie Oakley.

Impresario Pawnee Bill (Gordon William Lillie) presented a similar, rival Wild West show. Lillie launched *Pawnee Bill's Historic Wild West Show* in 1888. It starred his wife, May Manning, who was featured as a horseback sharpshooter. In 1908 Hickok and Lillie (who also ran a buffalo ranch) joined their creative forces to announce their *Two Bills Show*.

Above: Buffalo Bill's Wild West shows drew huge crowds of varied spectators.

Another Western showman, Joe Miller, founded the *101 Ranch Wild West Show* in 1905. The Miller family owned a huge 110,000 acre ranch in the Indian Territory of Oklahoma. Their neighbor, showman Gordon Lillie, inspired Joe Miller and his brothers to produce a Wild West show of their own. Joe was the star performer in the show, which also featured Bill Picket, Tom Mix, and even an aging Buffalo Bill.

A former soldier, scout, and bison hunter, Buffalo Bill Cody made his stage debut in Chicago, Illinois, in 1872. He starred alongside the legendary Texas Jack Omohundro. Cody's stage show made him an international celebrity and an American cultural icon. Mark Twain commented that his show gave his audiences "a last glimpse at the fading American frontier."

The Winchester Model 1873

A standard Model 1873 saddle-ring carbine, fitted with a twenty-inch round barrel. This gun was made in 1889.

SPECIFICATIONS

Caliber: .44-40

Barrel: 30 inch round, 24 inch round, octagonal, or round-octagonal, 20 inch round

Type: Tubular magazine lever-action rifle

Origin: Winchester Repeating Arms Co., New Haven, Connecticut

This rifle is a late-production Model 1873 Trapper's Carbine, made in 1909. It has a shortened sixteen-and-a-quarter-inch round barrel.

The Model 1873 offered three advantages over the Model 1866. First, it had a stronger frame. The original frame had been made of iron, but after 1884 was constructed from steel. Secondly, the 1873 had a dust-cover over the action. Thirdly, and perhaps most important of all, most 1873s were chambered for the .44-40 round (although other calibers were available). This was the same ammunition used by the Colt Frontier Six-Shooter, a version of the company's "Model P" type single action revolver and meant a man could carry one set of ammunition for these two popular firearms. This was particularly useful in the rigorous environment of the frontier. The Model 1873 was awarded the well-deserved title of "The Gun That Won the West."

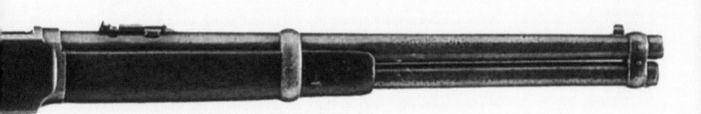

Like the Model 1866, the Model 1873 was sold in three versions. These were a musket with thirty-inch round barrel, a sporting rifle with a twenty-four-inch barrel (which could be round, octagonal, or combination round-octagonal), and a carbine with a twenty-inch round barrel.

There were the usual minor changes over the production run, which mainly involved modifications to the dust-cover. When production ended in 1919, around 720,000 Model 1873s had been sold.

The Rodeo

The idealized view of the cowboy and his professional skills that was first showcased in the Wild West shows was also perpetuated by the rodeo. This more realistic form of Western entertainment has become a durable and popular cultural phenomenon. To us, the rodeo seems like a window into the world of the traditional cowboy. But it actually pre-dates the days of the frontier by over a century. The first rodeos were held back in the early eighteenth century, when the Spanish ruled the West. These shows celebrated the authentic cowboy chores of tie-down roping, horse breaking, bronco riding (broncos are unbroken horses), branding, and team roping.

When the policy of Manifest Destiny emerged in the nineteenth century, the Western cattle business boomed. A huge amount of meat was required to feed the growing American population. Cowboys were in demand, and cowboying became a more valued profession. The rodeos of the later part of the nineteenth century celebrated the vital skills of these tough and resourceful men.

Rodeo became more widespread in the years following the Texas Revolution and the war with Mexico. As Harris Newgate wrote in 1858, "the vaquero of early days was a clever rider and handler of horses." Rodeo was a Spanish vaquero term, meaning "round-up" and did not acquire its modern meaning until 1916. The first rodeos were called "cowboy competitions," or "cowboy tournaments."

These early competitions were inspired by the skills cultivated by professional cowboys and cattle drovers. They soon became an important element of Western life. They were particularly popular with working cowhands as a means to demonstrate their skills and supplement their low wages. By 1851, rodeos had legal status in California, where the *Act to Regulate Rodeos* stated that each ranch should hold a rodeo each year. The first organized rodeo was held at Cheyenne, Wyoming, in 1872. Ten years later, Buffalo Bill Cody held the first commercial rodeo in Platte, Nebraska.

In 1888, the first professional rodeo competition was staged at Prescott, Arizona. This was the first tournament to charge an entry fee and award prizes. At this time, rodeo stars often performed in Wild West shows, like those of Cody and Lillie, as well as rodeos.

Almost from the beginning, rodeos were dogged by controversy around animal welfare, which was an issue for many people and animal welfare groups.

Above: Bucking bronco competitions grew from a cowboy's need to stay in the saddle under any conditions — it could be a matter of life and death in a stampede.

By the 1920s, rodeos were becoming increasingly fashionable, with trick roping being the most popular element of most shows. In 1923, Tex Austin hired the New Yankee Stadium for a ten-day event that awarded $50,000 in prize money. This was double the prize money offered at the Madison Square Garden rodeo in the previous year. Even during the Great Depression, rodeos maintained their large audiences, and many contestants earned between $2,000 and $3,000 a year. At the time, this was more than a teacher or dentist could expect to earn. The Texan promoter Col. William T. Johnson staged rodeos all over the United States and increasingly professionalized the sport. His events included bareback and bronco riding, steer wrestling and riding, and calf roping. By this time, rodeos had changed from a participation sport into a spectator event, and there was an increasing tendency towards general entertainment to be included in the format. In 1939 Gene Autry sang *"Home on the Range"* in the Madison Square Garden annual rodeo, and this tradition of mixing glitz and showmanship into the sport continued for decades. Under Autry's influence, rodeos also became increasingly patriotic events, especially during World War II.

After the war, the influence of individual promoters like Autry, Austin, and Johnson waned, and the sport of rodeo became increasingly regulated and controlled by large associations. Prize money also became much higher. In 1953, a total of $2,491,856 was available to be won. By 1983, this had increased to over thirteen million dollars. In 1976, Tom Ferguson became the first rodeo cowboy to earn more than $100,000 in a single year.

The 1970s were a period of unprecedented growth in the popularity of rodeos, and in 1989, the Texas Cowboy Hall of Fame was opened at Fort Worth, Texas. Despite this, the sport has continued to be dangerous, with a smattering of fatal accidents.

Participation in the sport of rodeo has now become a lucrative profession. Each year 7,500 contestants compete for over thirty million dollars in prize money in over 650 American rodeos. Although modern rodeo is only loosely based on the classic skills of the Western cowboy, it still requires extreme courage, strength, and expertise. Many rodeo events remain substantially unchanged. These include bull riding (the most popular event today), steer wrestling, calf roping, and bareback bronco riding. All of these activities are as potentially dangerous as they ever were. There are now several Rodeo Associations which run the sport, and cater to various niche groups. Although rodeo has always been a relatively inclusive sport, with participation by African Americans, Hispanics, and Native Americans from the early

Below: Steer-roping was also a crucial cowboy skill.

Right: Steer roping (also known as steer tripping) is a skill still showcased in rodeos. A professional steer roper can catch and tie an animal in around ten to fifteen seconds.

Right: Things don't always go according to plan, and rodeo work can be very dangerous.

days, these organizations now include the International Gay Rodeo Association and the All-Indian Rodeo Cowboys Association.

The profile of the participants has changed dramatically from the illiterate cowhands of the early years. Today, nearly a third of all rodeo riders have college degrees, and less than half of rodeo performers have ever worked on a ranch.

Cowgirl Rodeo Stars

The image of the female cowboy owed much to Annie Oakley's role as a sharpshooter in Buffalo Bill Cody's *Wild West Show*. Born Phoebe Ann Mosey, Oakley was born on August 13, 1860 in Woodland, Ohio. Her extraordinary abilities as a sharpshooter propelled her to become the first American female superstar. When Annie's father died while she was still a child, she began trapping and shooting game to help support her family. Gaining some notoriety for her fantastic marksmanship, she joined Buffalo Bill's *Wild West Show*, where she was billed as "Little Sure Shot." During her lifetime, Oakley taught over fifteen thousand women to shoot to defend themselves. She also became an early movie star.

Although cowboying remained an almost exclusively male profession, women were often involved in running family ranches. Some of these women also gravitated to the rodeo scene. By the 1920s, cowgirls performed in many rodeos as relay racers, trick riders, and rough stock riders. By 1928, at least one third of all rodeos had competitive events for women. Unfortunately, the 1929 death of the famous rodeo performer Bonnie McCarroll in a bronco riding accident caused many

Western shows to drop female events. Women were encouraged to participate as rodeo queens rather than athletes. When Gene Autry founded the Rodeo Association of America in the same year, it was created as an all-male entity.

When high unemployment struck in the Depression, more traditional gender roles were reasserted, and women became rodeo figureheads rather than participants. The restrictions of World War II were particularly devastating for rodeo women. Gene Autry held particularly conservative views about gender roles, and excluded women from all rodeos that he controlled. Effectively, Autry's influence meant that real cowgirls were banned from rodeos. In 1942, Fay Kirkwood staged an all-women rodeo in Bonham, Texas, but this was a showcase of women's rodeo skills, rather than a competitive event.

But there were always women that challenged their gender roles. Connie Douglas Reeves was born in 1901 in Eagle Pass, Texas. When the Great Depression forced her to leave law school, she became a teacher and riding instructor at Camp Waldemar at Hunt, Texas. It is estimated that Reeves taught over 30,000 women to ride at Camp Waldemar. She and her husband became sheep and cattle ranchers, but she continued to teach at the camp. In 1997, she was to become the oldest member of the National Cowgirl Museum and Hall of Fame. Reeves died in 2003, at the age of 101, when she was thrown from a horse. Reeve's hands-on motto was, "Always saddle your own horse."

In 1948, a professional women's rodeo association was finally created in San Angelo, Texas. The Girls Rodeo Association was founded with just thirty-eight members. This quickly grew to a membership of seventy-four. Many of these were women ranchers who had been forced to manage family operations while their husbands fought in the war. In its first year, the G.R.A. staged sixty women's events. In 1982, the organization was re-named the Women's Professional Rodeo Association. The Women's National Finals Rodeo is now held each year at the Cowtown Coliseum in Fort Worth, Texas.

Above: Rodeo has become a widely used cultural reference in different media.

Cowboys in the Movies

Opposite page: Errol Flynn appeared in four Western movies between 1940 and 1950. Although Flynn was best known for playing Robin Hood, his cowboy films were also popular.

The early Wild West shows etched the traditions of the working cowboy into the public mind, and were the forerunners of the Western movies that superseded them in the 1920s.

In fact, Western movies featuring cowboys were one of the first staples of the film industry, and they are still popular with today's cinemagoers. Cowboy characters were popular from the earliest days of the cinema, and their working environment and way of life became familiar to millions of moviegoers. The first movie cowboys represented a wide range of stereotypes, from the violent maverick to the honorable hero. The first cowboy movies of the silent era spawned several stars, including Art Acord, William S. Hart, Jack Hoxie, and Fred Thomson. Not all of these actors made it through to the next generation of talking pictures. In the 1930s, film sound technology made a new generation of clean-cut singing cowboys hugely popular. Gene Autry was the archetype of this new style of artist. Not only was Autry a fine singer, but he became heavily identified with his on-screen persona, and conceived his own "Cowboy Code." His basic credo was that a cowboy never shoots first, never takes unfair advantage, tells the truth, helps people in distress, and is always a patriot. Autry's clean-cut image suited the times, and propelled him to enormous popularity. Autry's lyrical character debuted in 1934's *Old Santa Fe*. He went on to make over a hundred films in his long and successful career, making the singing cowboy character hugely popular. Several actors subsequently adopted this persona, including Bing Crosby (in *Rhythm on the Range*, 1936), Tex Ritter, Bob Baker, and William Hopalong Cassidy Boyd.

In the 1940s, Roy Rogers succeeded Gene Autry as the singing King of Cowboys. He had played Autry's sidekick, Frog Millhouse, in many movies, but took his first lead in *Under Western Stars*. Rogers also went on to have a long and distinguished career on screen and television, and was one of the first stars to inspire a marketing phenomenon. He endorsed many products, including cowboy dolls, novels, and a comic strip.

Cowboy movies had an extremely positive effect on the film industry itself at this time, both economically and creatively. As the talkies surged onto the market, a whole new generation of cowboy movie stars began to hit the big time. They included such luminaries as Sunset Carson, Lane Chandler, Tom Mix (considered to be Hollywood's first cowboy megastar), and Gary Cooper. Cooper starred in

The greatness...the glory ...the fury...of the Northwest Frontier!

Universal-International presents

JAMES STEWART · ARTHUR KENNEDY
JULIA ADAMS · ROCK HUDSON

BEND OF THE RIVER

COLOR BY Technicolor

with LORI NELSON · JAY C. FLIPPEN · STEPIN' FETCHIT · Screenplay by BORDEN CHASE · Directed by ANTHONY MANN · Produced by AARON ROSENBERG

Above: Jimmy Stewart played several cowboy roles, including one in the 1952 film *Bend of the River*. The movie was directed by Anthony Mann and written by Western novelist Borden Chase.

1929's *The Virginian*. Considered by many to be the first modern Western (it was also one of the first talking cowboy pictures), *The Virginian* was directed by Victor Fleming. The film was the third screen version of Owen Wister's classic Western novel. Gary Cooper's character is a ranch foreman, beset by the all-too-familiar problem of cattle rustling. Manly, assertive, and decent, Cooper's character is one of the earliest film portrayals of the cowboy ideal.

The next round of cowboy actors from the 1940s and 1950s included Glenn Ford, James Garner, and John Wayne himself. The availability of many of the finest cinema actors ever to grace the screen made the 1930s, 1940s, and 1950s the Golden Era of Western movies, many of which revolved around cowhand characters.

John Ford's 1939 film *Stage Coach* is important for many artistic reasons, but is best remembered as the movie that projected John Wayne from B-movie Westerns to true stardom. Wayne was to become the most iconic movie cowboy of all time. Veteran film director Howard Hawks often cast Wayne as in cowboy roles. Hawks's 1948 movie *Red River* stars Wayne. It tells the story of the first cattle drive along the Chisholm Cattle Trail, fictionalized by writer Borden Chase.

Errol Flynn was another major Hollywood star whose career included a stint as a film cowboy. *Dodge City* (1939) was an early Technicolor movie in which he co-starred with Olivia de Havilland. Flynn plays a lone cowboy, with the action taking place in the Longhorn cattle center of the world, the last of the great cow towns.

In the 1950s, famous film cowboy Clint Eastwood began his career playing Rowdy Yates in the long-running television series *Rawhide*. It was his passport to becoming one of the most iconic movie cowboys ever. As his career progressed, Eastwood went on to play more complex and ambiguous cowboy characters in

Sergio Leone's so-called Spaghetti Westerns. Leone made an important contribution to the character of the screen cowboy in his movies by redefining their "look" as ragged and dusty rather than pristine and salubrious.

In the 1960s, the classic cowboy movie went through more difficult times and underwent several re-interpretations. One of the more questionable was 1965's not-very-funny comedy *Cat Ballou*. The movie tracks the adventures of a rancher's daughter (Jane Fonda) who hires a gunfighter (Lee Marvin) to protect the family acres. But the genre survived such indignities, and the 1970s saw the release of one of John Wayne's final offerings, the classic movie *The Cowboys*. When his ranch

Above: During his career in movie Westerns, Stewart wore the same hat and rode the same horse, "Pie."

Right: John Wayne played several cowboy characters during his long career, including the starring role in 1930's *Big Trail* and 1935's *The New* Frontier.

Left: In 1970's *Rio Lobo*, John Wayne's character Cord McNally returns several ranches to their rightful owners, and bankrupts the local villain, Ketcham.

Right: John Ford (right) made several cowboy films, or "horse operas," as John Wayne called them.

Below: Dean Martin played the drunken cowboy gunfighter in *Rio Bravo* (1970).

hands abandon him to join the gold rush, Wayne's character, Wil Andersen is forced to train up a group of schoolboys as cowhands so that he can drive his cattle the four-hundred miles to Belle Fourche, South Dakota.

Far from dying out, the classic cowboy movie has continued to evolve over the decades to reflect contemporary concerns and attitudes. The 2005 film *Brokeback Mountain* explores the complex sexual and romantic relationship between two (male) cowboys, and became one of the highest-grossing romance films of all time. Interestingly, the iconic bloodied shirts from the film are housed at the Autry National Center. Clean-cut singing cowboy Gene Autry founded the center in 1988 to explore the diversity of the people of the American West.

Below: Director John Ford's Western movies transformed John Wayne into the archetypical Western cowboy. He played variations on the role throughout his long career.

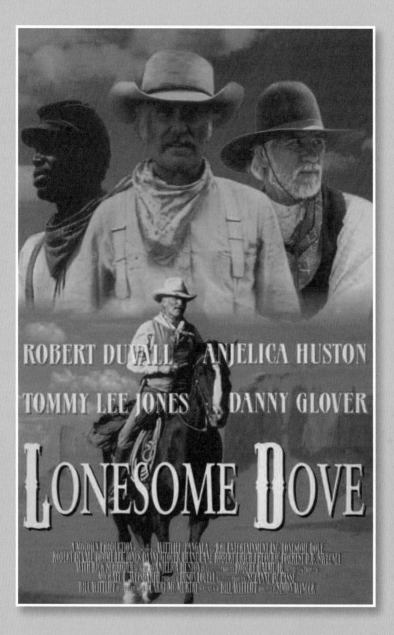

ROBERT DUVALL   ANJELICA HUSTON
TOMMY LEE JONES   DANNY GLOVER

LONESOME DOVE

Above: The story of *Lonesome Dove* revolves around the Hat Creek
Cattle Company and its owners and ranch hands. One of them, Joshua
Deets, is an ex-slave working as a cattle drive scout and tracker.

Left: In 1960's *Magnificent Seven*, seven cowboys-turned-
gunslingers defend a village from a Mexican bandit chief.
The movie was directed by John Sturges.

Cowboys on the Small Screen

From the early days of television, the cowboy also became a mainstay character of small screen entertainment. Early cowboy-inspired shows were the direct descendants of radio Westerns. Like their movie counterparts, these early television shows often featured so-called "singing cowboys," including Gene Autry, Roy Rogers, Rex Allen, and singing cowgirl Dale Evans.

The popularity of Western themed television shows continued for years, finally peaking in 1959, when cowboy-inspired programs occupied no fewer than twenty-six primetime slots.

The very first network television Western, *Hopalong Cassidy*, aired on June 24, 1949. Based on Clarence E. Mulford's clean-cut cowboy character, the original shows

were re-edited B-movies. But these were so successful that the NBC network commissioned some original half-hour episodes. These were immediately successful, rating seventh in the 1949 Nielsen ratings. A radio version was also launched. The show's longstanding success inspired several other cowboy shows for children, including *The Gene Autry Show* and *The Roy Rogers Show. The Roy Rogers Show* ran for a hundred episodes between 1951 and 1957. This NBC show also starred Roger's real-life wife, Dale Evans. Dale Evans wrote Rogers's signature theme, *"Happy Trails."*

NBC's *Bonanza* was another iconic cowboy series. Running for fourteen years between 1959 and 1973, the show followed the fortunes of the Cartwright family, who lived on the one-thousand-square-mile Ponderosa ranch in Lake Tahoe, Nevada. *Bonanza* was the first hour-long serial to be shot in color, and starred Pernell Roberts and Lorne Green. Between 1962 and 1971, NBC ran a second cowboy series, *The Virginian,* alongside *Bonanza*. The action of

SPURR
HOLLYWOOD

Best Wishes
Tom Mix

Opposite page: Tom Mix starred in over one-hundred-sixty cowboy movies in the 1920s. He was named an honorary Texas Ranger in 1935.

Left: Clayton Moore starred as the Lone Ranger. His catchphrase was, "Hi-ho, Silver!"

The Virginian was set in the 1880s, and revolved around the business of another large ranch, the Shiloh. James Drury played the Shiloh's tough ranch foreman (and the eponymous Virginian), while Doug McClure remained his loyal top hand, Trampas, for the entire series. Alongside both shows, NBC ran a third ranch-based series, *The High Chapparal*. The series was set in the Arizona Territory of the 1870s, and featured Leif Erickson as rancher Big John Cannon. The show ran for four seasons between 1967 and 1971.

Left: Gene Autry began his career as "Oklahoma's Yodeling Cowboy".

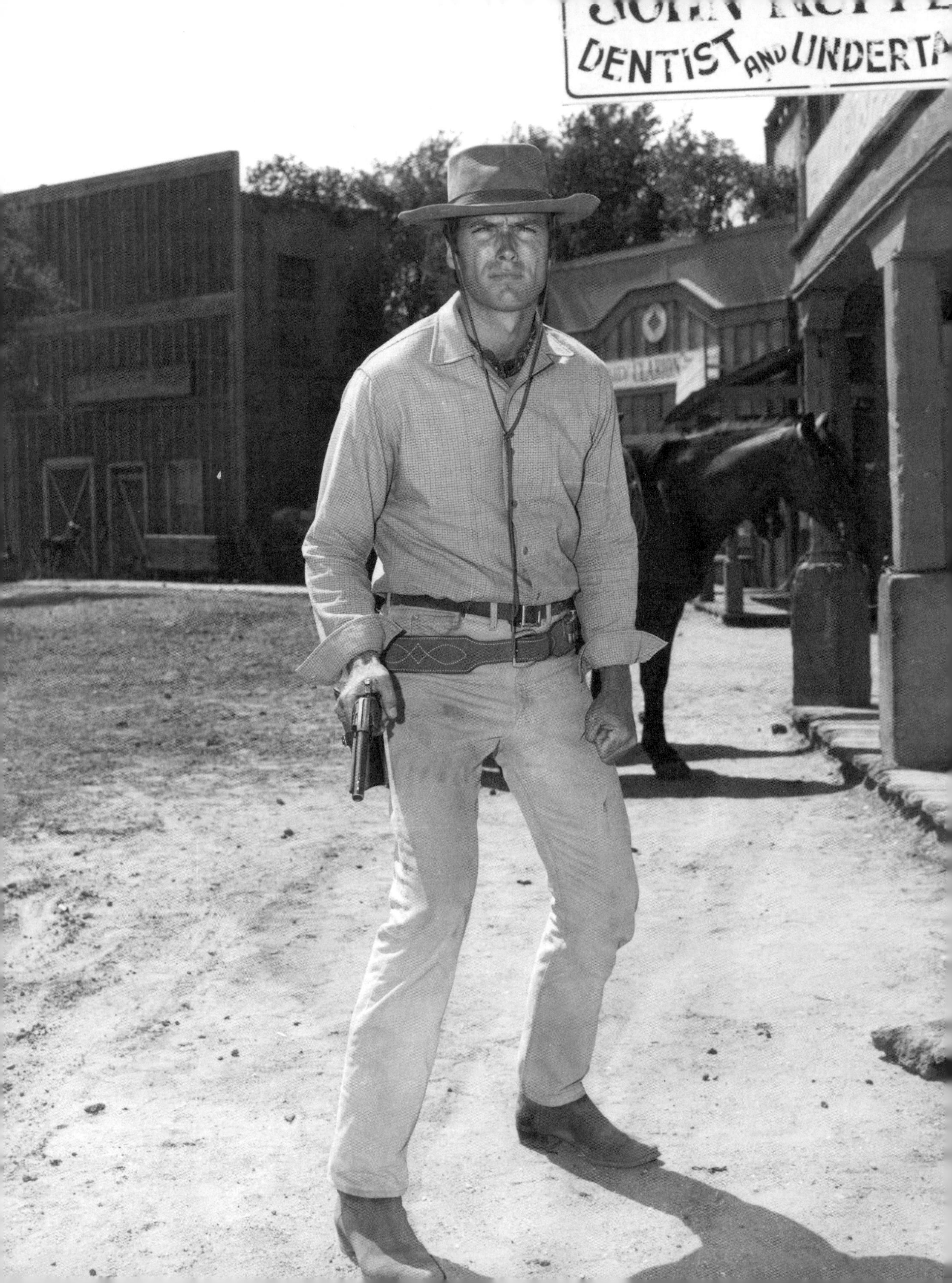
DENTIST AND UNDERTA

In 1959, the CBS network had launched its own cowboy series, *Rawhide*. The program is now most famous for launching Clint Eastwood's career. Eastwood played the role of Rowdy Yates (who he later described as "the idiot of the plains"). Set in the 1860s, *Rawhide* portrays the challenges faced by a group of cowboys driving their herd along the Sedalia Trail. On the series, about twenty-five drovers (of whom Yates is one) control three thousand head of cattle. This is probably more men than would have been used in real life.

Along with regular series, the networks also produced a number of made-for-television movies featuring cowboy characters. A good example of this would be 1991's *Conagher*. Based on Louis L'Amour's novel, the story revolves around a ranching family and their fight against cattle rustlers, Indian attack, and marauding gangs.

Above: *Gunsmoke* was an iconic television western series of the 1950s. It starred James Arness as Marshal Matt Dillon, policing an area dominated by ranchers.

Opposite page: Clint Eastwood starred as cowboy Rowdy Yates in the 1950s television series *Rawhide*.

Left: Roy Rogers became the most heavily marketed and merchandised singing cowboy of all time.

Right: James Garner starred as cowboy Bret Maverick in ABC's television series, *Maverick.*

Above: Dan Blockner, Lorne Greene, and Michael Landon starred in *Bonanza*. The action centered on a family-run ranch.

In all its different forms, the Western has not only been a foundation of American popular culture, but has also played a huge part in shaping it. Starting in the written form and evolving into movies, radio, and television, Westerns have been a staple of American entertainment for nearly two centuries. The formats and revenue generated by the Western genre have influenced a huge swathe of popular culture, and continue to do so. Westerns have not only revealed a fascinating aspect of American culture and history to an enthralled world, but have also helped to remind us of the origins of American life itself.

Above: The cast of *The High Chaparral*, with
Leif Erickson in the center.

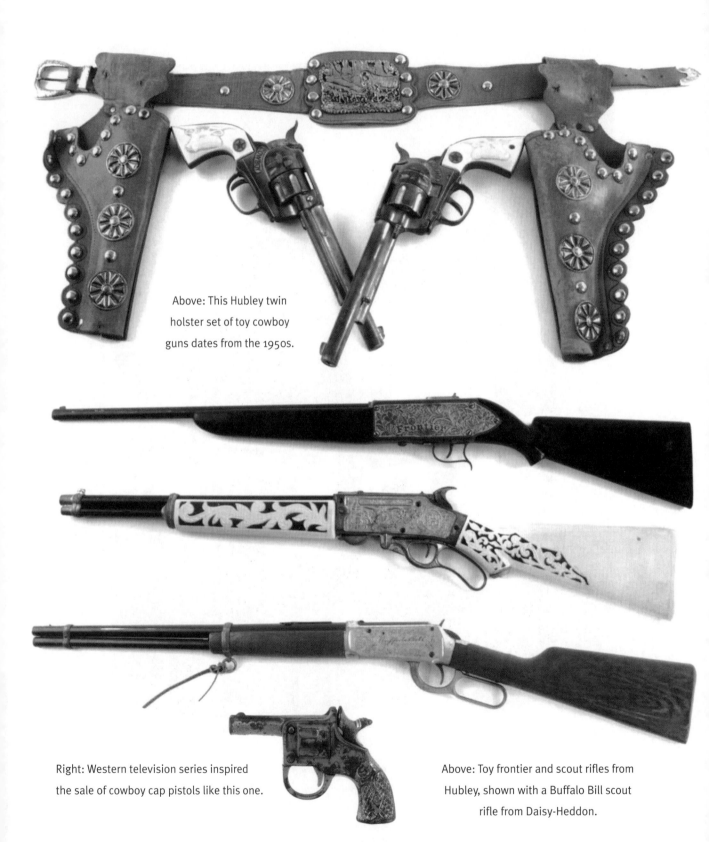

Above: This Hubley twin holster set of toy cowboy guns dates from the 1950s.

Right: Western television series inspired the sale of cowboy cap pistols like this one.

Above: Toy frontier and scout rifles from Hubley, shown with a Buffalo Bill scout rifle from Daisy-Heddon.

Left and right: Toymakers Marx and Esquire made these two versions of bounty hunter Josh Randall's gun.

Below: Toy Derringers were popularized by television Westerns.

Above: The 1950s cap gun craze led to a sudden flourishing of different firing systems.

Acknowledgements

J.P. Bell, Fort Smith, Arkansas

Johnny C. Brumley, Texas

The Buffalo Bill Historical Center, Cody, Wyoming

Judy Crandall, Eagle Editions, Hamilton, Montana

Colorado History Society

Walter Harder, Kamloops Secondary School, British Columbia.

Patrick F. Hogan, Rock Island Auction Co., Moline, Illinois

Stuart Holman, Auctioneer, Cincinnati, Ohio

Andrew Howick, MPTV, Van Nuys, California

Kansas City Historical Society

Jerzy Miller, Lazy C.J. Cattle Co., Texas

Donna Morgan, Director, Callaway Family Association, Texas

Emily Lovick, Fort Smith National Historic Site, Fort Smith, Arkansas

The National Archives

Kathy Weiser, Legends of America, Lenexa, Kansas